Liberalism

Short Histories

Agenda Short Histories are incisive and provocative introductions to topics, ideas and events for students wanting to know more about how we got where we are today.

Published

The Campaign for Nuclear Disarmament
Martin Shaw

Conservatism
Mark Garnett

Deglobalization
Edward Ashbee

Liberalism
Jonathan Parry

Social Democracy
Eunice Goes

Thatcherism
Peter Dorey

The War on Terror
Andrew Thomson and Rubrick Biegon

Liberalism

Jonathan Parry

agenda
publishing

First published in 2025 by Agenda Publishing

Agenda Publishing Limited
PO Box 185
Newcastle upon Tyne
NE20 2DH
www.agendapub.com

ISBN 978-1-78821-804-7 (hardcover)
ISBN 978-1-78821-805-4 (paperback)

British Library Cataloguing-in-Publication Data
A catalogue record for this book is available
from the British Library

Typeset in Minion by Patty Rennie

Printed and bound in the UK by TJ Books

EU GPSR authorised representative:
Logos Europe, 9 rue Nicolas Poussin, La Rochelle 17000, France
contact@logoseurope.eu

Contents

Preface

I am very grateful to Alison Howson for commissioning this book. It has given me the chance to develop a general argument about British Liberalism that I have wanted to make for some time. Chapters 1–3 draw on several of my research publications on nineteenth-century Liberalism, but all the chapters also rely on the work of many other scholars, not all of whom there is room to mention in the bibliography. Modern British political history is fortunately still a thriving field of study.

This project has also allowed me to reconnect with the twentieth-century history of the Liberal Party, which was one of my first historical enthusiasms. When I was growing up, the Liberals were my team. My parents were enticed to join the party by the vivacity of Jo Grimond. Not having been to university, they embraced his emphasis on the importance of working out their own intellectual and moral positions and rejecting stale conventional thinking parroted by a complacent political establishment. Liberal raffles and jumble sales played a large part in my childhood in Dover in the late 1960s and 1970s. Local Liberal social life implanted in me the idea that political activity was really a means through which thoughtful, humane and public-spirited people could enjoy each other's company. Adult politics, therefore, has been something of a disappointment.

I have followed the usual convention of capitalising "Liberal" and "Liberalism" when applying these words to the Liberal Party and its political impact, but otherwise using lower case. This is not always an easy distinction to draw.

I am particularly grateful to Duncan Brack, Richard Brent and Peter Sloman, who were kind enough to give me detailed comments on a first draft of this book. It is much better for their input, and so much changed that they are in no sense responsible for whatever errors and misunderstandings remain. I have also benefited from the online archive of back issues of the *Journal of Liberal History*, expertly edited by Duncan for several decades now. Vivian Bickford-Smith and Richard Fisher gave me very insightful and supportive feedback on a later draft. I owe something also to all the people with whom I have talked about Liberal politics over the years, particularly John Lotherington and James Raven, but also the late Conrad Russell, with whom I overlapped many years ago when I was a young lecturer in the History Department at King's College London. He could certainly never be accused of bowing down to convention.

Introduction

This book is a short history of political Liberalism in modern Britain. It defines British "Liberalism" in terms of political practice rather than theory. Its subject is the British Liberal Party, and its successor the Liberal Democrats. It focuses on these parties' public presentation of their aims – their policies, campaigns and arguments – rather than their mechanical aspects (their organization, electoral fortunes or voting base). In this book, "Liberalism" means the ideas and visions put forward by Liberal politicians and by those journalists and writers who advocated the party's causes. Liberalism is probably the most widely used word in the political lexicon. It has been defined in a dizzying variety of different ways. This reading of the term is appropriate because this book stands in a historical series on ideas in British politics.

Politicians are rarely abstract thinkers, and they almost never have the luxury of applying coherent principles to specific problems. They operate within very powerful constraints: of party pressure, popularity, precedent and cost. When we study the politicians of the Liberal Party, we cannot hope to find one single "Liberal" ideology, in the sense of a theoretically coherent set of principles. A party which agrees on everything will never collect enough electoral support to compete for power. The political historian must be sensitive to chronology and context: strategies go in and out of fashion, and opportunities and demands for political action are stronger at some times than others. When Liberals were in government, Conservative opponents tried to persuade voters that they were destroying the national fabric; as a result, Liberals often disagreed about how much reform was prudent. We can recognize the compromises of the political process but still think that ideas matter in politics. We can see recurring tendencies and patterns over time.

This book argues that British Liberalism is best defined as a prejudice against *concentrations of power* – in the hands of governments, landlords, corporations or religious bodies. Liberals have worried that excessive powers in such hands have jeopardized the good government of the nation or the freedom of individuals. Structural defects in the political constitution have needed amending. Economic vested interests have appeared to acquire too much political or social influence. Monopolies have obstructed access to resources. Publicly funded authorities have seemed to lack public accountability. Minorities have suffered discrimination. Powerful thought-systems may threaten freedom of expression.

Vested interests, and abuses of power, are always with us: they are a feature of the human condition. This Liberalism has been a practical political movement, not a utopian ideology seeking perfection on earth. It has operated by rallying opinion in favour of proposals to challenge specific abuses. Its definition of a vested interest is an entrenched advantage that a significant number of people find offensive enough to persuade them to support a political campaign against it. Well-drafted legislation can regulate and check many vested interests, but it can never remove all social unfairness. Utopian philosophies require potentially revolutionary social restructuring. Liberals, on the other hand, have historically set their faces against revolutionary disorder and put their faith instead in the British constitution. This necessarily limits the amount of social change they have advocated.

One major theme of political Liberalism has been criticism of the accumulation of powers by central government. This criticism has assumed different forms over time. The Liberal movement started as a challenge to the power of the Crown: the monarch and his or her ministers. This challenge required reforming parliament in the hope of representing public opinion better. Liberals also defended the principle of religious pluralism within the constitution, and local government power against central bureaucracy. Liberals have generally argued that good government involves devolving powers to accountable bodies that enjoy local public confidence. In the twentieth century, they also came to advocate sharing national sovereignty with international authorities, where these were best placed to tackle specific global problems.

Liberals have always insisted that this defence of freedom and pluralism was not just compatible with the strong rule of law but its only viable foundation in the long term. Popular consent strengthened the legitimate authority of government. Active political debate revealed social grievances that required redress. Effective political processes were essential in convincing people to obey the law rather than to pursue violent alternatives. Many Liberals have claimed that political participation helps to develop ideas of citizenship, not least because it teaches realism about what politics can and cannot achieve. Popular disillusionment and passivity encouraged vested interests to assert themselves: Gladstone warned in 1877 that they made "a night of it" whenever the public slept (Parry 1986: 170).

Some Liberal leaders were happy for the party to define its agenda around the demands that emerged from the political process, inside and outside the party. Others were more determined to shape it by firm leadership and their own choice of legislative priorities. Liberal governments usually operated through a mixture of leader preference and backbench pressure. Some individual Liberal politicians had an intellectually developed approach to policy that might be called a personal ideology. But Liberals have also been more willing than both the other main parties to welcome internal party freedom of debate about the principles and the timing of reform measures.

In particular, British political Liberalism has never been an ideology of the free market. Most individual Liberals have felt that taxes should not be oppressive, that checks on the free flow of goods are inefficient, and that bureaucratic planners can easily damage economic creativity. Some have even developed these views quite rigidly. But political Liberals have also always realized that free markets can create concentrations of power: that employers can bully employees, that powerful corporations can exploit customers, that rich men can acquire secret political influence. Liberals have always seen both the market and the state as essential agents in politics, while remaining conscious that both might tempt powerful interest groups into dangerously antisocial behaviour. Liberal initiatives on economic matters have been much more concerned to tackle political failings and imbalances than to uphold economic theories.

Liberal history

Liberalism's heyday was the period before 1914, and so Chapters 1–3 examine the strategic objectives of Liberals and their party in government between 1830 and the First World War. The Liberal Party emerged logically out of the 1832 Reform Act: its driving principles and its organizational form both followed from the provisions and effects of that Act. The 1832 Act was a political watershed, but it did not emerge from nowhere, and many of the preconditions for a liberal politics already existed in eighteenth-century Britain.

Since 1688, parliament had imposed effective checks on the power of the monarch and his or her advisors. The 1689 Bill of Rights underwrote the principle of frequent and free elections to parliament, and declared that the ministers of the Crown would not tax British subjects or keep a standing army without parliamentary approval. It listed established and "ancient" legal rights, including the right of petitioning to parliament for the redress of grievances. A strong legal culture already defended individual property rights, and the principle of religious toleration was widely accepted. After 1688, monarchs' ministers had to command the confidence of the House of Commons, which meant that they had to limit their demands on it for tax revenue. This was less painful because of British economic success, which allowed the state to secure massive bank loans on the security of its future tax receipts. The global reach of the eighteenth-century British economy produced general confidence in liberal capitalism and the social benefits of national and international commercial exchange. Most commentators felt that the British constitution secured a balance between effective authority from above and consent from below, and that constitutional liberties underpinned national economic success. In the propaganda wars against revolutionary France in the 1790s, this balanced British constitution was constantly contrasted with the extremism of a republic, in which the regime claimed absolutism, in the name of the people, while delegates could be swayed by waves of popular passion.

On the other hand, the French Revolution, and rapid urbanization and industrialization after 1800, produced enormous social and intellectual strains, which exposed defects in constitutional arrangements. Parliament seemed inactive and slow to respond to grievances. The French wars unleashed inflation and made high taxes unpopular. Tariffs on imported foodstuffs were rigidly high; there were periodic food riots. Most local government remained in the hands of landed elites who had little scope or talent for innovation. Rural pauperism seemed out of control. Policing was rudimentary and the army was frequently used to quell disorder. Middle- and working-class radicals campaigned for parliamentary reform. Many members of the propertied elite also came to see that some adjustment of the relationship between parliament and people was essential to legitimize state authority and order. A social and political crisis in 1829–30 brought in a new coalition government of men willing to pass a Reform Act.

The 1832 Reform Act aimed to give government that legitimacy. Its importance lay not so much in what it did as in what it removed. It removed most of the "nomination" boroughs controlled by individual local property-owners, which had given governments a parliamentary majority irrespective of movements of public opinion. It allowed a competition for parliament in most constituencies, which forced parties to organize to win elections. It created a mechanism by which pressure groups at local level could lobby effectively for legislative changes at Westminster. So it created a national political conversation about the demands made by the most popular pressure groups. Westminster politicians rapidly separated out into two parties, one of which was instinctively sympathetic to giving these pressures a hearing, and the other instinctively resistant to them.

In the 1830s, therefore, a Liberal Party emerged, supported by voters who identified with the interests of towns, of Protestant minorities and of Irish Roman Catholics. Traditionally, some historians were reluctant to call this force a Liberal Party at this early date, preferring to use the name "Whig" – the word used to describe the opposition politicians who had come into power in 1830 and passed the Reform Act. It was once common to argue that a Liberal Party only emerged in 1859, when a small group of former Peelite Tories, including William Gladstone, formally joined the "Whigs" (Douglas 2005). However, the governments of Lord Melbourne (1835–41) and Lord John Russell (1846–52) were party governments, which some people called Whig and some called Liberal. Their policies needed to please their backbench MPs who argued that the concerns of towns, religious minorities and Ireland needed more attention. Gladstone brought something new to the party, but he also adapted to fit its culture. Moreover, it remained as badly disciplined, in modern terms, after 1859 as before.

Between 1830 and 1914, Liberal governments were in power for nearly two-thirds of the time. They set the direction and tone of politics. Even when Conservative governments passed important legislation, they were responding to pressures that groups of Liberals had mobilized; most famously when Conservatives repealed the Corn Laws in 1846 and passed the 1867 Reform Act, but also when Jews were allowed to enter parliament in 1858 and when a bold Irish Land Purchase Act was passed in 1903. This is not surprising, because the Liberal movement was a very broad affair, involving extra-parliamentary organizations such as the Anti-Corn Law League as well as parliamentary activity. Between 1846 and 1874, the Conservative Party never had a parliamentary majority, so its three brief governments depended on the acquiescence of some Liberal MPs. After 1886, the Conservatives won three electoral majorities, but one reason for this was their coalition with Liberal Unionists who defected from Gladstone's Liberal Party. The only Conservative majority government between 1830 and 1874, Peel's government of 1841–6, likewise gave high office to two defectors from the Liberal Party: Sir James Graham and Lord Stanley (later Lord Derby).

Chapters 1–3 discuss the three main areas of Liberal governing practice. In each case the aim is to explain the continuities and changes in Liberal assumptions over time, while also signalling some of the party's more important tensions and disagreements, as far as possible in the space available.

Chapter 1 is about the evolution of representative politics between 1830 and 1914: the development of a more democratic constitution through successive Reform Acts. It argues that this development naturally followed from the principles on which the Liberal Party was formed, even though most early Liberals would have been horrified by the full democracy that eventually transpired. Once the party organized itself around the claim to respect genuine popular grievances, it proved impossible to resist that evolution. Aristocratic Liberals originally supported Reform primarily to widen the number of genuine social interests represented in parliament, and to strengthen executive government and the rule of law by managing parliamentary demands sensitively. But many of them were always conscious that a propertied parliament would not make essential legislative changes without "pressure from without" of various sorts: to repeal the Corn Laws, to improve the rights of disadvantaged religious groups, to enhance trade union protections, to extend the franchise itself. All these pressures affected the direction of policy. Most Liberals also quickly realized that the most important mechanism for connecting elite and popular politics harmoniously was party. Organizing politics around party loyalties had several benefits: it disciplined MPs to pass a legislative programme, it created approved channels for voter participation in politics, and it helped to sustain the influence of the established social elite while providing a ladder for aspirant politicians from other classes. But it also meant that party interests necessarily shaped the process by which the constitution was democratized.

Chapter 2 discusses Liberal approaches to the economy, to taxation and to foreign affairs. The army and navy remained the costliest items of government spending. Although some Liberals wanted Britain not to intervene in global politics, most of them considered a strong foreign policy essential strategically and economically. Tax and spending policy was also affected by Liberal suspicion of the power of domestic economic interest groups. In the 1830s, many Liberals claimed that politics was still being poisoned, as in the eighteenth century, by various vested interests: that well-connected individuals could acquire political offices for private financial gain rather than public service, while West Indian slaveowners could buy their way into parliament to prop up slavery. After 1832, Liberals also increasingly criticized a "landed interest" whose defence of agricultural protection seemed antisocial. The argument emerged that the state would secure popular loyalty most easily if it appeared "disinterested" in economic and social policy, rather than controlled by a self-serving class. Some Liberal and Conservative politicians admired the systematic theories of laissez-faire economists, who counselled against any state attempts to distort markets. However, Liberal governments were always willing to endorse state activity when it seemed to promote the general interest (as in education) or to address a popular demand. Once the franchise was extended in 1867 and 1884, the claim that the state was still a malevolent nest of elite vested interests lost its remaining plausibility, while powerful popular lobbies demanded government action of various sorts. There was an inexorable and gradual move towards what some have called the "New Liberalism": of targeted state activity to deliver particular social goods, specifically pensions and Poor Law reform, funded by a taxation system that was justified to voters on grounds of social fairness. And defence policy continued to be the main driver of extra spending and new taxes.

Chapter 3 considers how far Liberal governments took note of the demands and grievances of different religions, localities and British overseas possessions. The Liberal Party was committed to the principle of incorporating diverse religions within the constitution, and then to tackle their expressed grievances. The Nonconformist conscience powerfully shaped Liberal attitudes on many domestic and foreign issues. On the other hand, elite Liberals wanted to maintain the state's moral authority, which had traditionally relied on a close association with the Established Church of England. This led to a tense balancing act, especially in education policy. These tensions were addressed mainly by developing the principle of local self-government: after 1870, for example, locally elected school boards decided how much Bible teaching their schools should offer. In these ways, more activities were brought within the remit of publicly accountable politicians without increasing the powers of central government. Liberal governments were relaxed about trusting elected local bodies with power in Britain, because local political and religious elites with broadly liberal inclinations could usually dominate these bodies.

The great problem for Liberal governments in Ireland was that a similarly liberal governing elite never emerged, except in small pockets. Irish politics seemed dominated by more uncongenial warring groups: ultra-Protestant absentee Tory landlords, Catholic bishops with close links to the papacy, lawless Fenians funded by American republicans, small-town MPs of dubious financial probity and demagogues with nationalist tendencies. Liberal governments tried several strategies for responding to Irish popular grievances, but they did not risk dismantling the colonial structures of Irish government that they inherited in 1830. The same problem shaped Liberal policy on empire. In the West Indies and India, the power systems through which imperial adventurers had imposed their will on local populations were entrenched, and Liberal governments made only intermittent attempts to reform them. In the newer colonial settlements, Liberals had to decide how far to support principles of local self-government. In Canada, they inaugurated a relatively effective liberal politics, but in South Africa and New Zealand self-government produced conflict between white settlers and the indigenous population, raising awkward questions about British responsibility.

In the early twentieth century, the rapid growth of organized labour in Britain confronted Liberals with the dilemma of dealing with such a large and potentially powerful sectional interest. They were willing to offer trade unions significant legislative concessions, while still claiming to hold the ring equitably between capital and labour interests. Then the accidental interaction of major events in the 1910s – war, labour shortages, strikes, franchise extension, internal party conflict – persuaded millions of trade unionists that the Liberal Party was no longer for them. Between 1914 and 1924, the party lost its status as the driving force of British politics. After 1924, it was a lame third runner in a two-horse race for electoral victory, behind the Conservatives and Labour. The increasing importance of the language of class in interwar elections led many Liberals who distrusted union power to support the Conservative Party instead, against "socialism".

From the 1920s, Liberals' vote share was squeezed, and the other two parties wooed their supporters. Both of them drew extensively on liberal values and attracted a large number of ex-Liberals. The five most prominent Conservative leaders between 1924 and 1964, Stanley Baldwin, Neville Chamberlain, Winston Churchill, Harold Macmillan and R. A. Butler, all had close family affiliations with Victorian Liberalism or, in Churchill's case, had served in a Liberal cabinet. The first Labour cabinet, in 1924, included ex-Liberals Noel Buxton, Richard Haldane and C. P. Trevelyan, while Roy Jenkins and Tony Blair later spoke frequently about their debts to the Liberal tradition.

Chapter 4 considers the limited options that a centre party has had in a first-past-the-post system. The Liberal Party took up the cause of proportional representation partly out of self-interest, as the only way it might get back into power. But it did so also from a belief that the Conservative and Labour parties represented divisively sectional approaches to policy, between which some structural constitutional compromise was necessary in the national interest. Between the 1920s and 1950s, politics turned mainly on the battle between capital and labour, and most voters were not interested in the Liberals' nuanced positions. Between the 1950s and 1980s, they achieved some success by contrasting their good sense and moderation with the apparent extremism of one or both parties. However, since then, the emergence of a large welfare state, the decline of the major industrial unions and the growth of a post-industrial and highly globalized economy have all lessened the distance between Conservative and Labour approaches to the economy, and made the economic centre ground more crowded. When Liberal parties have been able to attract attention for their economic policy arguments, these have usually been for their *political* rather than their *economic* impact. These include the attempts of Lloyd George and Keynes in the 1920s, and of Jo Grimond between 1956 and 1964, to rebrand Liberalism as the energetic and moral political force that a badly led country needed.

Chapter 5 argues that the Liberal Democrats' distinctiveness in modern politics still lies in their criticism of excessive central government power. It traces their significant involvement in the legislation of the 1990s and 2000s to introduce devolution and to protect civil liberties and human rights. It also discusses Liberals' consistent concern with European and international cooperation, and their hostility to the argument that "sovereignty" can safeguard the country's destiny. All these critiques of government power have had a political importance beyond their intrinsic significance, because Liberals have tried to use them to disrupt the established political system.

Theory and practice

Liberalism has many potential meanings: political, economic, legal-cultural, philosophical. They are easily mixed up. In economics, liberals seek to show that markets allocate resources with maximum efficiency. Philosophers argue – as John Stuart Mill did – for the freedom of the individual as an ethical principle. Michael Freeden has produced the best introduction to the variety of ways in which liberalism can be defined theoretically: as a historical theory of human progress, an ideology or a philosophical view of the world (Freeden 2015). This book does not aim to retread that ground. It does not explore the development of liberalism as an economic or philosophical position.

My approach here aims to complement his: to define British Liberalism instead as what political leaders have done and said. I have added occasional discussion of political arguments made by Liberal theorists, but in the specific historical context for which those arguments were intended.

I am certainly not the first to define Liberalism as a political rather than an economic doctrine, and my argument has benefited particularly from two predecessors (Russell 1999; Fawcett 2015). Whatever originality this account possesses lies in my attempt to run this theme systematically through the political history of the party. The task of defining Liberalism in this way is easier than it once was, because British historians, including me, have been analysing the languages and thought of political leaders for several decades. Political discourse is sometimes slippery and trivial, but the most effective political leaders can often articulate powerfully coherent dreams and visions. Moreover, these often have an afterlife, because future generations of activists like to refer to them, to draw on them and sometimes to reinvent them. The most effective political initiatives expand a specific issue into a powerful moral cause by bringing it alive to different groups of supporters. The Liberal argument for free trade between 1903 and 1906 combined arguments based on the free market, fair taxes, humanitarianism, social reform, international peace and Liberal history going back to the 1840s. A similarly rich set of arguments and historic parallels was used to make the case for Irish Church disestablishment in 1868–9. This is politics at its most artful.

This book claims that Liberal leaders such as Lord John Russell, William Gladstone, David Lloyd George, Jo Grimond and Paddy Ashdown are better guides to political Liberalism than theoretical writers such as J. S. Mill or T. H. Green. It argues that politics has its own rationale, and that politicians take up bodies of ideas for specific purposes, rather than allowing works of theory to set their policy agendas for them. Asquith and Grimond are often said to have been influenced by Green, not least because they both attended the Oxford college at which he taught, although in Grimond's case long after Green died. Perhaps they were: they were intelligent men who read a vast amount. Hundreds of Victorian Liberal pundits made interesting and rich contributions to national political debate. We know much more about these than was once the case, so there is no longer any excuse for elevating Mill or Green into a small elite of Liberal "thinkers" who have had a transcendental impact on the party's definition.

Green's writings, like those of most intellectuals, are interesting less as influences on future policy than as responses to the issues of his day: to the concerns of the 1870s about temperance, university extension and freedom of contract. Mill and Green contributed to contemporary politics in important but specific and limited ways. Mill's constitutional opinions, set out in 1861, reflected his worries about the impending Second Reform Act. His aim was to advocate the principle of democracy while trying to marginalize the opinions of many of those whom it would enfranchise. We should also recognize that the desire of modern Liberals to celebrate past heroes has perpetuated Mill's posthumous career. Each president of the Liberal Democrats is given a copy of his most famous work, *On Liberty*, on assuming office. Yet its concerns were overwhelmingly not with party politics but with preserving intellectual individuality from conformist social pressures. Grimond suggested that Liberals should reread it annually for stimulation but immediately criticized its confused and outdated terminology (Grimond 1963: 35–6).

Studying the history of political thought offers an excellent intellectual training, but its students run the risk of assuming that supposedly representative "thinkers" must have some undefined significance on practical politics. A very influential group of writers on the British Empire has drawn up a charge sheet against "Liberalism" for legitimating the misgovernment of nineteenth-century imperial subjects (Mehta 1999; Mantena 2010; Elkins 2022). They have used a few abstract works by Mill, his father and T. B. Macaulay to construct an allegation that nineteenth-century liberal ideology condoned the exclusion of native imperial subjects from power in the name of their "improvement". These historians extrapolate confidently from theory to political practice, because they do not think that they need to offer any proof that these texts shaped what politicians thought and did. Chapter 3 offers an alternative reading of Liberal imperial policy which pays more attention to politicians' views.

Modern commentators who try to connect Liberal theory with Liberal practice have made one assumption which, this book suggests, has caused them particular problems. They have exaggerated the hold of classical economic doctrines on nineteenth-century politicians (mainly because they have not read enough early Liberal political history). They have therefore also exaggerated the extent to which Liberal assumptions needed to be rethought during the twentieth century. Most early Liberals, and many subsequent ones, deeply respected the general principles of market economics, but their respect fell a long way short of an ideology that constrained their freedom of political initiative.

As recent surveys of postwar Liberal thought by Kevin Hickson and Tudor Jones show, most contributions to party debate have felt the need to begin by constructing a theoretical opposition between "classical" and "social" (interventionist) Liberal positions, in order to place themselves somewhere on that scale (Hickson 2009: 2; Jones 2011). But they also show that no modern Liberal denies the need for intervention, so constructing this opposition seems unnecessary. Indeed the academic and former MP David Howarth has ridiculed the amounts of emotional energy expended in elevating into a matter of principle a mundane question about whether public services are best run by market or administrative processes, when the answer obviously depends on circumstance, and when it would be much more productive to debate issues of freedom, democracy and inequality (Howarth 2007: 3–4). Ramsay Muir pointed out in 1934 that no Liberal government – from 1832 onwards – had ever practised laissez-faire; on the contrary, they had been responsible for most state interventions in the economy (Muir 1934: 169). Roger Fulford, one analyst of Liberalism, reminded his readers that no economic arrangements are "natural"; they all rely on particular legal protections, such as the principle of limited liability (brought in by a Liberal government in 1856) (Fulford 1959: 51–2).

The Liberal Party's institutional ethos as a reformist party has given it no choice throughout its history but to respond to public grievances about economic conditions, often with interventions of various kinds. Many free-marketeers have joined the Liberal Party *assuming* that it was a temple for the worship of their principles, partly because of academics' continued insistence on the importance of a "classical" tradition. A lot have left, disillusioned; some have stayed. Arthur Seldon, a major early influence on the free market think tank the Institute of Economic Affairs, was a Liberal. The hedge fund manager Paul Marshall funded a Liberal Democrat think tank, but then left the party, supported Brexit on free market principles and bought several right-leaning media outlets, including GB News and *The Spectator*. Liz Truss was once president of the Oxford University Liberal Democrats. The Conservative Party, from Peel to Truss, has provided a more congenial home for laissez-faire doctrinaires because it has less need to respond to pressures from outsider social groups demanding interventionist redress.

Historians of political Liberalism have also perpetuated a related and equally problematical theoretical model, in which a "negative" view of liberty gave way to a "positive" one in the "New Liberal" era around 1900. On this reading, the assumption that government could promote liberty best by interfering less was superseded by an awareness that a rounded idea of human liberty required it to interfere more. Undoubtedly central government took on more tasks at this period, but this process was triggered much less by changes in Liberal argument than by institutional and electoral factors, including voter pressure, civil service policy-making expertise and concerns about Britain's "national efficiency" in the face of great power competition. Chapter 2 argues, instead, that Liberal policy-making has always been "social", or "positive" in the sense of trying to check the excessive power of particular political or social interests, which have been defined differently at different times. Early nineteenth-century Liberal policies – of economic retrenchment and lower tariff barriers – were aimed at specific political targets. Attacks on high taxes and official sinecures sought to reduce the unpopularity of the governing regime and remove the imputation of "old corruption" from which it suffered. The battle against agricultural protection was an attack on class privilege. In the 1890s and 1900s, some writers proclaimed themselves "New Liberals" by defining themselves against old classical economists such as Adam Smith and utilitarians such as Jeremy Bentham. Their argument was that Smith and Bentham had seen social relations in mechanistic terms, whereas it was now possible to organize the state around a higher politics founded on ethical principles. Yet it is unwise to assume that Smith and Bentham gave earlier versions of Liberalism their philosophical basis. "New Liberals" ignored the many previous Liberal critiques of a materialist politics. In truth, their abstract philosophical arguments had a mundane purpose: to attack the continued political influence of Gladstonian tax-cutters. Their particular ethical focus was only one of several influences on Edwardian Liberal policy (Sloman 2015: 24–35; Meadowcroft 1995).

This book suggests that the most distinctive Liberal and Liberal Democrat interventions on economic issues have been, and continue to be, shaped by political aspirations rather than narrowly economic ones. After all, politicians can do less to reshape the economy than is often claimed, except by adjustments to taxes, tariffs and organizational structures which all necessarily have a political purpose as much as an economic one. Liberals have often argued for using the power of the state to rein in the excessive power of economic interests. At the same time, their fundamental distrust of concentrations of power has made most of them suspicious of central bureaucratic planning.

A direct connection can be traced between the tendency to define Liberalism as an abstract defence of laissez-faire and the many attacks on liberalism in current political debates. At an intellectual level, this attack has been led by an influential school of "post-liberal" British and American writers. Patrick Deneen in the United States, and John Milbank and Adrian Pabst in Britain, blame liberals for the triumph of globalization, lax controls on immigration and the breakdown of traditional family values. They claim that a triumphant global free market has concentrated real power in a few wealthy corporations and produced disturbing levels of income inequality, while wealthy liberal elites have damaged social and moral cohesion through excessive concern with personal self-fulfilment, for example on matters of gender identity (Deneen 2018; Milbank & Pabst 2016). In other words, they see "liberalism" as a double-headed phenomenon, resting on the "neoliberal" turn in right-wing economic thinking since the 1980s, and the ethical individualism of John Stuart Mill on social matters. Some British Conservatives have adopted a similar position and used it to explain the failure of the Conservative government of 2019–24. Former Home Secretary Suella Braverman pronounced four days after the 2024 election that the Conservatives had "governed as liberals, and were defeated as liberals" (Braverman 2024).

This book does not aim to enter this debate, except to make the point that "Liberalism" in British politics has not meant what its contemporary critics allege it to mean. Political Liberalism, as discussed here, has always urged the need for a better balance of social power, and has been as concerned with the state and civil society as with the market and the individual. One post-liberal, Adrian Pabst, called for the state–market dichotomy to be supplemented by a focus on "the intermediary institutions of civil society, which give people agency – professional associations, profit-sharing businesses, trade unions, universities, ecological groups and devolved government" (Pabst 2017: 501). This is in fact a description of traditional Liberal politics. The more nuanced "post-liberal" writers have always recognized that their approach must build on Liberal achievements (Goodhart 2012). Yet nuance has got lost in current debate. Francis Fukuyama had a point when he interpreted the election of Donald Trump in November 2024 as the consequence of this distortion of definitions of liberalism in contemporary discourse. Anti-liberals, he argued, have been allowed to get away with reducing "liberalism" to the two dogmas of "neoliberalism" and what he calls the "woke liberalism" of unlimited personal ethical choice (Fukuyama 2024).

All ideologies, including "post-liberalism", can be criticized as utopian, which is why politicians need to handle them with care. The social trends to which "post-liberals" object rest on very strong foundations: a global capitalist system, a complex state bureaucracy and a legal-political framework in which the defence of rights is deeply embedded. If politicians are to be judged on their success in dismantling them for something better, they are very likely to fail. That is another reason why it makes more sense to study political ideas through the practice of politics itself: to anchor our analysis of Liberalism in an assessment of the mundane readjustments that experienced politicians have thought that they might stand a chance of achieving.

PART I

1830–1914

1

Liberalism and the constitution

The 1832 Reform Act established a new system of two-party politics. At this time, most party organization took place in individual constituencies and aimed at winning a particular election contest. Once elected, MPs expected to enjoy a considerable degree of independence in their voting habits, and governments could not take their loyalty for granted. However, by the time that Lord Melbourne formed his government of 1835, after the election early that year, it was clear that MPs at Westminster were dividing into two camps, one of which – Melbourne's supporters – was much more sympathetic than the other to demands for further reform, from urban Britain and from religious minorities. Journalists did not always agree on how to describe the political tribes at Westminster. The specific term "Liberal Party" to describe the reformist camp was widely adopted by commentators from the mid-1830s, although other names, especially "Reformer" and "Whig", also continued in use, reflecting the importance of the Reform Act and the role of the old Whig aristocratic party in passing it (Coohill 2011). The same was true for the Liberals' opponents, increasingly known as the Conservative Party but still often called Tories.

The 1832 Act was primarily a renewed attack on excessive Crown power, by making parliament better able to express "public opinion". It also attacked the bribery and corruption which self-interested lobby groups had used to buy their way into parliament. Reformers argued that the Act would strengthen the social structure and protect Britain from revolution, but that leaders would now have to show consistent willingness to take popular grievances seriously. The Whig aristocrats behind the Act saw themselves as public-spirited leaders of that type. They had no problem with the representation of real local interests, but they wanted parliament to reflect better the diversity of the economy. The Tory party, whose power base the Act attacked, argued that parliament would now be buffeted by waves of pressure from whichever interest groups were able to mobilize for further changes.

Meanwhile many Reformers alleged that parliament remained biased towards propertied interests. Indeed the Conservative Party won the 1841 election, suggesting that Reform had not gone far enough. Reform-minded Liberals quickly grasped that parliament itself would never be a perfect debating chamber in the absence of "pressure from without": pressure from constituencies and interest groups, to force it to be more zealous.

Throughout the century, Liberals constantly faced a dilemma about how far to engage with extra-parliamentary groups, ranging from religious minorities to trade unions, which claimed to be oppressed or ignored. The votes of these people were essential to Liberals at elections. But the party risked appearing to be their prisoner: to surrender to vested interests itself. This was awkward enough in the 1840s and 1860s, but the problem got worse in the 1880s, because some of these pressure groups took up niche causes that Conservatives claimed were unpopular. In 1891, Liberals grouped their demands into a "programme" which formed the basis of their appeal at the 1892 election. Conservatives alleged that Liberals had become "faddists", touting a series of specialized promises and relying on programmatic politics to manufacture an artificial coalition of support for them.

Groups of Liberals periodically defected to the Conservatives, particularly at points of crisis such as the 1830s and 1880s (and again in the 1920s). By the early twentieth century, many Conservative politicians were ex-Reformers who had drawn the line at concessions to particular interest groups. Lord Stanley left the party in 1834 over its attack on the Irish Church; Joseph Chamberlain in 1886 over Gladstone's Home Rule policy; Winston Churchill in 1924 over Liberal support for "socialism". The Conservative Party, which might have remained a narrowly landed party, became a broader coalition of grumpy liberals from different eras.

Whenever concerted popular pressure developed for the inclusion of more people within the parliamentary franchise, Liberals generally found it difficult to argue against the principle (although many of them quibbled about specific proposals). This Liberal drift to support further democratic reform was the fundamental cause of the further Reform Acts of 1867 and 1884. Liberal leaders backed Reform also in the hope of revitalizing their own agenda: of giving a momentum to

Liberal legislative politics which parliament alone could not give. Lord John Russell and William Gladstone saw Reform Acts as cathartic acts of reconnection with "the people" and legitimations of the Westminster political process.

The Reform Acts of 1867 and 1884 did indeed reinvigorate party politics by forcing parties to respond to new voters and their new demands. They established the basic structure of modern politics: an electoral competition for power between two nationally organized parties. But this reinvigoration also benefited the Conservative Party, because it turned out that many voters did not like the activist politics that the Liberal Party promoted.

In the decade before the First World War, the party system turned on a series of well-publicized battles about tariffs, taxes, peers and people. Political debate was as great a national spectator sport as Edwardian football or cricket. Another issue was the emergence of politicized organized labour, in the shape of a Labour Party in 1906. This was the latest of the sectional interests that Liberals had to work out how to accommodate. When war broke out in 1914, the Liberal Party had been in power continuously for over eight years. Its aim continued to be to keep Labour MPs as subordinate partners, so that both together could still mobilize effectively against their Conservative opponents.

The 1832 Reform Act and the new politics

The Reform Act claimed to be corrective and restorative: to remove abuses that had crept into the system of parliamentary government that had been established since 1688. The aim was not democratic reform but *parliamentary* reform: to improve parliament's ability to do its job of connecting the people and the government. It rested on the principle that a healthy polity allowed the expression of popular grievances through elections, and required responsive political leadership. The Act removed 143 "rotten borough" seats from the Commons, nearly all of which returned MPs who had bought their way in and represented only the private interests of themselves or their backers. From now on, in principle, each constituency should represent some real interest, and its electorate should have a genuine connection with the place; non-resident freemen were disfranchised.

The Reform Act was the creation of the Whigs, the aristocratic network led by Lord Grey which came into government in 1830 after decades of opposition during the reigns of George III and George IV. During that time, they developed the argument that excessive private influence and ministerial corruption had betrayed Britain's constitutional heritage. Governments were abusing their power through heavy taxation, the enlargement of an unaccountable civil and military bureaucracy, the invasion of civil rights by repressive legislation and discrimination against Catholic and Protestant religious minorities. In the 1810s and 1820s, many Whigs, radicals and independent country gentlemen came round to the view that some kind of "Reform" would improve parliament's ability to reduce taxes, to preserve civil liberties and to promote government accountability.

Portrait of Lord John Russell

Source: Penta Springs Limited/Alamy Stock Photo.

The case for Reform was about authority as well as liberty. The social crisis of 1829–30 included major riots in rural Kent, known as the Captain Swing riots. Propertied politicians were uncomfortably aware of disorder, pauperism and crime. Younger Whigs such as Lord John Russell (born in 1792) stressed the weakness, sloth and unpredictability of the executive government: its inability to respond effectively and systematically to public grievances. The Reformers' main charge against the Tory prime minister, the Duke of Wellington (1828–30), was his feebleness and sectionalism. They claimed that his premiership was inactive because it doubted its popular standing. Popular confidence would permit stronger national government pursuing nationwide legislation on clear principles, including reform of the Poor Law and criminal law to improve popular moral discipline. As Russell said in 1831: "it is upon law and government, that the prosperity and morality, the power and intelligence, of every nation depend" (Parry 2006: 50–1).

The Act was not intended to challenge the social status quo; its authors expected that men of property would continue to govern the country at national and local level. Russell argued that the bill did not damage the aristocracy, merely those aristocrats "who do not live among the people, who know nothing of the people, and who care nothing for them – who seek honours without merit, places without duty, and pensions without service" (Parry 1993: 87). He blamed the French Revolution on the irresponsibility of that country's decadent, pleasure-loving aristocracy. Whig-Liberal leaders expected that public service would be met by popular gratitude and posthumous fame. The best monument to this way of thinking is the 133-foot-high statue of Lord Grey in the middle of a busy Newcastle square. In the same way, it was hoped that giving all large manufacturing towns their own MPs would establish a secure channel for popular campaigns, making them "at once salutary and safe". Russell blamed the 1819 riots in Manchester on the fact that "there was no authority to which [the populace] could conform, or from which they could derive instruction" (Parry 2006: 51–2).

Nothing about the Reform Act was democratic. A property franchise was maintained in the counties. In the towns which were given separate borough representation, the standard entitlement was the occupation of a property which had an annual rental value of at least £10. Parliamentary seats were not allocated by population numbers, and not every town was given separate representation. The thinking, rather, was that the booming Lancashire cotton interest, for example, should have enough seats to allow it to influence parliamentary debates. The redistribution of parliamentary seats aimed not to realize a mathematical ideal but to make the country's major economic and social interests feel that parliament was responsive (Spychal 2024: 31–3). The concept of "public opinion" was novel and fashionable in the 1820s, but it was never precisely defined. The terms of the Reform Act were a necessarily rough attempt to allow it more voice.

The best answer to those who argue that the Reform Act was unimportant because it was undemocratic is the political development that followed it. It did more than any other single change to create the idea of a national political conversation. Debate in parliament quickly came to be shaped by pressures from outside it. The first was the enormous weight of petitioning for the abolition of slavery in the empire, which made abolition inevitable in 1833. After that, three main types of extra-parliamentary pressure quickly emerged. One, driven mainly by the large towns, was for the removal of protective tariffs and especially the Corn Laws, discussed in Chapter 2. A second was from British Protestant Nonconformists for the removal of the discriminatory legislation against them, and a third, even more powerful, was from the Irish Catholics led by Daniel O'Connell, which are both considered in Chapter 3.

The Irish controversies were responsible for the political crisis of 1834–5, which led to the resignation of those members of the Reform coalition who disliked the implications of this new politics. These included Grey himself. After that crisis, the label "Liberal Party" was increasingly used to describe those MPs who accepted the principle of respecting Irish Catholic grievances. Lord Melbourne's government of 1835 – in which Russell, as Leader of the House of Commons, dominated domestic affairs – was founded on this principle. Whether aristocratic politicians liked it or not, the survival of Liberal government would now be determined by electoral organization in the constituencies, particularly in the towns, on which the parliamentary party quickly became dependent for a majority. Meanwhile the Conservatives mobilized rural and Anglican propertied Britain against these alarming threats. The Reform Act produced dividing lines around which both parties would cohere for several decades.

Reform and mid-Victorian Liberal debate

The electoral victory of the Conservative Party in 1841 reflected the power of landowners and the Church of England in county and rural borough seats. This alone convinced some Liberals that the Reform Act had not done enough to represent the most powerful industrial economy in the world. On the other hand, Peel's Conservative government collapsed in 1846 in the crisis over his proposal to repeal the Corn Laws. In the 20 years after 1846, Liberals were usually in government, because the Conservative Party, having opposed repeal, lacked enough seats in the Commons to form a majority government.

These events dimmed the radicalism of most mid-Victorian Liberal MPs. They were in office, and there was little popular pressure on them for any major changes. In the 1850s and 1860s, the global dominance of Britain's manufacturing products produced widespread prosperity accompanied by low taxes. Moves towards free trade, particularly the repeal of the Corn Laws in 1846 and of the Navigation Laws in 1849, made it much more difficult for radicals to allege that economic policy was still controlled by vested interests.

Liberal confidence in existing constitutional arrangements was encouraged by comparisons with continental countries. The 1848 revolutions in Europe seemed to end in instability, failure and reaction, and most European regimes still appeared autocratic, heavily centralized and – owing to the presence of large standing armies – militaristic. The British, by contrast, appeared to form a successfully integrated political community. After 1848, a consensus view emerged that individual conscience, civic virtue, hard work, enterprise and respect for law had made Britain a great commercial power and saved it from socialism, plunder and anarchy (Parry 2006: 59–64). As Chapter 3 argues, self-government became seen as the natural right of those Britons who had emigrated to Australia and Canada. Rhetoric of this kind suggested that Britain did not need any further constitutional reform. The great beneficiary of this line of argument was Viscount Palmerston. As a young man, Palmerston had served for 20 years as a junior minister in pre-Reform Tory governments. He had moved into the Liberal camp in 1830 after accepting the need for Reform, and developed a reputation as a successful and popular foreign secretary (see Chapter 2). However, his instincts remained those of a Liberal Tory of the 1820s: that a policy combination of liberalism abroad, Catholic Emancipation in Ireland and a lowering of tariffs and of taxes on middle-class Britons would give government enough popularity to make further Reform unnecessary. He, and these assumptions, dominated British politics between 1850 and 1865.

When the journalist Walter Bagehot wrote *The English Constitution* in 1866–7, his main aim was to discourage utopian arguments that the mid-Victorian political settlement should be overhauled just because of its theoretical imperfections. He was not impressed by the alternative representative systems on offer: in the United States, where a rigid constitution based on an unworkable degree of separation of powers was helping the country to tear itself apart over slavery; and in Napoleon III's France, which seemed subject to the whims of an individual and of crude plebiscites. He claimed that the existing British constitution produced a better balance between stability and liberty than any major reform of it was likely to do. The cabinet formed an essential buckle between government and people, between Crown and parliament. Parliament worked, despite the eccentricities of individual MPs, because it discussed important issues, was open to popular pressure, articulated widely held views and helped to educate the public. It was the only institution which could harmonize the country's contending interests. He was particularly hostile to the idea of equal representation and to increasing the weight of the unpropertied or uneducated.

One consequence of this complacency was to put Russell at an increasing political disadvantage. Although a younger son of the Duke of Bedford, a leading Whig landowner, he had no independent wealth himself, and lived, by aristocratic standards, in a relatively small house in Richmond Park (now a tea room) lent to him by Queen Victoria. He was MP for the City of London. As prime minister of the 1846–52 Liberal government, he started after 1848 to advocate a modest new Reform Bill, for several reasons. He thought it would enthuse his party; he disliked the suggestion that he was indifferent to the concerns raised by Chartist agitators in 1848; he hoped that a new Reform Act would give momentum to his broader reform agenda (for education, public health and Ireland); he was also becoming conscious of the threat posed by Palmerston as a potential alternative leader of Liberal MPs. But when he sought to bring forward the issue, he was said to be premature, restless and selfish, risking exciting the public mind unnecessarily.

Similarly, when he introduced resolutions calling for a "general and compulsory" system of national education in 1856, on the grounds that the education system in England was backward compared with "the other enlightened nations of the world", he was decisively rebuffed. The Leeds Nonconformist Edward Baines claimed that he was advocating the despotism of Berlin and Vienna (Parry 1996: 159–60). These criticisms made it easier for Palmerston to supplant him. Palmerston was prime minister from 1855 to his death in 1865 with one brief break, because his lack of zeal about legislative activity suited most MPs, Conservative as well as Liberal, better than Russell's more programmatic politics. Reform bills were introduced occasionally but not passed.

However, more radical Liberals disliked this chauvinist complacency and the lack of legislative activity. One million Chartists had marched on Kennington Common in 1848, and while Chartism then died away, the hopes that had underpinned it did not. Chartism articulated the old radical argument that the country would be fairly run only if "the people" had the right to vote. The £10 occupation franchise in the boroughs seemed a deliberate class policy, excluding working-class voters. Quite how to define "the people" was a matter of debate, but after 1848 most radicals agreed to demand household suffrage: that each male who headed a household should vote on that household's behalf. The MP Joseph Hume brought in his "Little Charter" – of household suffrage, the secret ballot, triennial parliaments and fairer representation of large towns – in June 1848.

Though pressure for household suffrage abated during the complacent 1850s, it was only a matter of time before it resurfaced. As the lack of interest in revolution in Britain suggested, many British working men were now hard-working, self-reliant and respectable; why should these manly qualities not justify receipt of the franchise? They were also better educated in public affairs: cheap newspapers were distributed nationally after the railway revolution and the repeal of the stamp duties in 1855. Liberal writers started to accept that good character – common sense, self-discipline, restraint and concern for others – rather than restrictive property qualifications should now determine the right to vote. From 1857, high-profile radical MPs John Bright and Richard Cobden promoted parliamentary reform forcefully, and most Liberal MPs sitting for sizeable borough seats were publicly committed to

Reform after 1859, in response to local pressure. They suggested that embracing artisans within the constitution would improve political morality and national integration; conversely, excluding them would risk them thinking and acting as a separate class. In 1866, William Gladstone lamented that the "influence of separate classes" was now "too strong"; a truly national and integrated politics in "the public interest" was urgently needed (Hansard 27 April 1866: 144).

In the 1860s, a serious-minded monthly periodical press emerged, in which young Liberal university graduates such as Frederic Harrison and John Morley found a congenial platform for their reformist arguments. These "lights of liberalism" sketched out a vision of Liberal politics based on an altruistic coalition of "brains and numbers" (Harvie 1976: 113–14, 149–50). They admired the ethos of artisans and hoped that they could be led to prefer virtuous causes to issues of pounds and pence. This hope derived from the willingness of Lancashire cotton workers to support the cause of the North in the American Civil War of 1861–5, despite the damage that the war did to cotton imports and therefore their living standards. Artisans' approval of the cause of Italian unification was also encouraging; it seemed to suggest that they shared Liberal academics' own vision that politics could celebrate the cause of human brotherhood.

These university Liberals expected John Stuart Mill to be the intellectual leader of this movement. Mill even became an MP for the Westminster constituency as an independent in 1865, without needing to canvass, to pay for his own expenses or to toe a party line. He openly told working-class voters that some of their class lied, that the secret ballot was a bad idea and that his heterodox opinions on religious subjects were none of their business. Mill supported democracy as a basic ethical principle, but he was also concerned that it might make working-class economic interests politically dominant. So his purpose, in *Considerations on Representative Government* (1861), was to hedge universal suffrage around with various qualifications that would give "brains" enough equality with "numbers" to shape political debate. These included extra votes for those with university degrees and a scheme of proportional representation so that the voice of the educated minority was assured a place in parliament. His hope was that an intellectual clerisy could prevent shallow and conventional mob opinion drowning out healthy intellectual inquiry and freedom of thought. As his previous work, *On Liberty* (1859), showed, his primary concern was the defence of the latter.

Arguments of this type were based on precisely the idealistic aspirations that Bagehot warned against. But, while idealistic, Millite radicals were not utopian. They were inspired by the influence that intellectuals (including writers in the *Edinburgh Review*) had had on the social legislation of the 1830s. Moreover, they were annoyed at the amount of money in politics, and specifically the ability of "plutocracy" to buy its way into representative assemblies in Britain, the United States and France. Constituencies seemed happy to elect local nonentities who scattered money about but were not interested in big issues and lacked the administrative ability to tackle national problems. In 1867, the *Westminster Review* remarked that it "is because [the plutocratic] class and the peers have legislated imperfectly for England that the call for Reform is so loud and general". If rich MPs, such as the "railway interest" which lobbied for benefits for train companies, were able to skew legislation in their favour, working men would have a better case for following suit. If brains and numbers did not ally, money concerns would rule (Parry 2017: 49–54).

When Palmerston died at 80 in October 1865, Russell, now a peer, became prime minister again, at the age of 73. His Reform Bill of 1866 expanded the borough franchise to include most of the urban upper working class. He and William Gladstone, now the Leader of the House of Commons and Russell's obvious heir, also wanted to reinvigorate Liberal politics. Both men criticized Palmerston's legislative inertia; Gladstone had begun as a Conservative and protégé of Sir Robert Peel but had moved into the Liberal Party in the 1850s in the hope of persuading it to adopt a vigorous programme of administrative reform and economy. They expected that Reform would pressurize parliament to be more active, as it had been in the 1830s.

Yet Liberal Party MPs could not agree on the details of Reform. There were agonized discussions about how to draw the line between men of good and bad character. Russell's 1866 Reform Bill was defeated by Liberal dissidents, leading to his resignation and a minority Conservative government that could not avoid bringing in its own Bill. Complex political manoeuvring in 1867 produced a surprisingly radical new Reform Act, on the basis of household suffrage in the boroughs, but little change in the counties. The Conservative leader in the House of Commons, Benjamin Disraeli, had proposed household suffrage hedged round with many qualifications to protect minority and propertied interests. Radical MPs then struck out nearly all the latter.

By delivering the core Radical demand, for male household suffrage, the 1867 Reform Act seemed to answer the main query about the legitimacy of state authority. Radical ideas of popular sovereignty appeared to be reconciled with the descent of authority from the Crown. The Act was accompanied, in 1872, by the introduction of the secret ballot for elections. This was a declaration that the independent voter was to be protected from undue vested interest pressure, whether from landlords and employers or from class-conscious trade union agitators. The Ballot Act was one of many Acts passed by Gladstone's government of 1868–74: the Liberal Party tackled the perception that much-discussed measures had been delayed for too long with bills on education, Ireland, army reform and university tests. Gladstone, now prime minister, hoped activity would discipline MPs and keep them out of mischief. He wanted to organize the Liberal Party around the "vital principle of . . . action" (Parry 1993: 252–3). He also retained Peel's belief that rigorous reform to purge impurities within the state would show ex-Chartists that the state was not a nest of old corruption. His remarkable energy, restlessness and religious self-belief also made legislative activism a psychological necessity for him – a personal vocation and a duty to God as well as a service to political stability.

All this legislation, passed by the first activist majority government since the 1830s, produced the same Conservative electoral reaction as it had then. The 1874 election delivered the first majority Conservative government since 1841. Propertied voters saw Liberal activism as an alarming taste of democratic things to come. Radicals had begun to moot land reform. Anglicans felt threatened by the concessions made to Nonconformists and Irish Catholics (discussed in Chapter 3) and even more threatened by their dissatisfied demands for more. Brewers disliked the temperance legislation of 1872.

Yet the Conservatives had not won the popular vote. They triumphed because of the electoral system in the British counties, where they won 169 seats against the Liberals' 50. Their gamble in 1867, when their Reform Act had shielded the existing county representation from Liberal tinkering, seemed to have paid off. Mill's vision of Reform, on the other hand, had failed: after 1874 there were more complacent, conservative bankers and businessmen in the Commons than ever.

The creation of a modern party system

Between 1874 and 1886, the structure of British politics was transformed. The electorate rose fourfold between 1865 and 1886, to nearly six million, mainly because of a Third Reform Act in 1884 which was accompanied by a major restructuring of the electoral map. Both main parties developed a mass nationwide organization in the hope of winning elections. Ever since, British politics has been dominated by the conflict of two national party machines. The trigger for these changes was Liberal anger at the Conservative election victory of 1874 on the basis of narrow and mainly rural support.

Reduced to opposition, the Liberals acted as if parliament did not represent national opinion and sought to mobilize public opinion outside it in a number of dramatic ways. In 1876, Nonconformists and radicals organized protests against the atrocities meted out by the Ottoman government to its Christian Bulgarian subjects, and against Disraeli's Conservative government for its apparent acquiescence in that misgovernment (Shannon 1963). Having retired as Liberal leader only the year before, Gladstone could not resist re-entering the political fray to support this "virtuous passion". These years saw the full flowering of "the people's William", helped by the ability of the late Victorian economy to produce and distribute his image en masse on commemorative postcards, ashtrays, plates, teaspoons and Conservative-made chamber-pots. His occasional hobby of tree-felling on his Flintshire estate became one of his trademark symbols: in the 1880 election, posters proliferated of Gladstone the woodman cutting down a poisonous Conservative tree (Hamer 1978: 36–41). His speeches were reported verbatim in the national and provincial press. His Midlothian campaign of 1879–80 gave him a profile and legitimacy that the parliamentary Liberal leadership could not challenge, and he became prime minister again after the party's election victory that year.

Meanwhile in 1877 a new body, the National Liberal Federation (NLF), had met in Birmingham to encourage the development of popular Liberal Party organization throughout England and Wales, but also with the aim of agreeing some new policies. The Birmingham radical Liberal Joseph Chamberlain put himself at the head of this movement, suggesting that this popular assembly of activists could direct public opinion better than a confused and complacent parliament dominated by Tories. After the Liberal victory of 1880, Chamberlain, who had only become an MP in 1876, was put straight into the cabinet as the representative of constituency activist radicalism.

After 1880, Liberals were bound to press for further parliamentary reform, and the obvious logic was to make the electoral arrangements in the counties conform to those in the boroughs, by extending male household suffrage throughout the country. County seats now contained over three million urban voters who happened to live outside traditional borough boundaries, whether in small towns, expanding suburbs of larger ones or mining villages. It was not possible to deny their suitability for the vote, especially as the existing working-class electorate had not abused the privilege. So the 1884 Reform Act brought household franchise to the counties. As before, Liberals presented this change as a way to smooth class tensions and divisions and to replace sectional and exclusive politics with a properly national and inclusive system. Reform might weaken the grip of the Conservative squirearchy, but it would not damage the stature of propertied MPs who sought to be responsive representatives, and indeed it might bolster legitimate propertied influence. There was also a particular case for enfranchising agricultural labourers, given rural tensions in the 1870s and the formation of the Agricultural Labourers' Union in 1872. Enfranchisement would avoid class polarization: it would ensure that parliament responded equitably to the grievances of farmers and labourers and would create a level playing field between them and landlords (Parry 1993: 280–86).

The wider ambitions of the 1884 Reform Act were to free the counties from Conservative rule, or, to put it more altruistically, to install participation, openness and responsibility where Liberals had previously seen only Tory ruling class arrogance, injustice and complacency. As Chapter 3 shows, towns increasingly had effective drainage and schools, bathhouses and art galleries, mostly provided at a modest cost to ratepayers. Rural areas usually lacked these. It seemed obvious that replacing irresponsible magistrates with elected authorities would make rural local government more accountable, more competent and more active, improving standards of education and health and increasing popular respect for the propertied classes. Later, in 1894, a Liberal government created rural district councils and parish councils.

The Act was a step change towards democratization. Indeed the home secretary, William Harcourt, was privately appalled by such "a frightfully democratic measure", but the political elite could do nothing about its inexorable logic (Saunders 2013: 155). Equalizing the franchise across the nation destroyed the logic of treating county seats differently from borough ones. Although the formal distinction survived, constituency boundaries were restructured much more dramatically than in 1867. Many small boroughs were disfranchised, and counties and towns were divided into single-member constituencies. The number of seats in large towns greatly increased. In 1879, 192 of 282 English borough seats represented towns with a population of under 50,000; in 1886, only 73 of 226 did. Alarmists assumed that most of these constituencies would be dominated by poor voters: that the voice of the masses would predominate over minority interests. For that reason, Millite academics led by Leonard Courtney pushed for proportional representation, which might also protect the Protestant minority in Ireland. But their case foundered on opposition not just from radicals, who thought it anti-democratic, but also from Conservatives, who felt that it would give control to local activists in party caucuses and so radicalize the whole political system. The leading Liberal Lord Hartington argued that the true safeguard against extreme opinions would continue to be "the liberal character of the Legislature" as a whole (Parry 1993: 285).

The effect of these changes on the Liberal Party cannot be separated from the impact of the dramatic political crisis of 1885–6 over Irish Home Rule, discussed in Chapter 3, which split the party badly and ended Liberal hopes of dominating politics. Most Liberal property-owners now became Liberal Unionists rather than support Gladstone's Irish scheme. Gladstone lamented that "nine-tenths of our wealth is gone". In 1886, only 59 Liberal MPs were landowners; by 1892, only 15 per cent of county magistrates supported the party (Parry 1993: 307).

Another reason for the growth of national party organization was the Liberals' 1883 Corrupt and Illegal Practices Act. It was the most effective of nineteenth-century legislative initiatives against electoral corruption, setting strict limits for candidate spending and ruling out treating, although agents soon became adept at bending the law to maximize spending. Elections became increasingly dependent on professional organizers, local volunteer campaigners and central party assistance. The NLF became the backbone of Liberal Party organization; the great majority of local associations joined it. Constituency activists became used to discussing policy matters.

The NLF's annual conferences adopted an increasingly detailed legislative agenda. In 1887, it agreed to support Welsh Church disestablishment and the reduction of the powers of the Lords, in 1888 one man one vote and ground rent taxation, and in 1889 Scottish disestablishment and a local veto on the sale of alcohol. At first, Gladstone paid little attention to this programme, hoping to continue to organize the party around the single-issue politics of Home Rule. This became impossible after the Irish leader Parnell was brought down by a divorce scandal in 1890. Irish Home Rule became even less electorally popular than before. The NLF's 1891 conference at Newcastle adopted a dozen specific policy proposals. The Liberals narrowly won most seats at the 1892 election: the Conservative leader Lord Salisbury argued that their plurality rested on a mere 150 votes in 8 constituencies, collected by the various sectional policy bribes that made up the "Newcastle Programme". Gladstone returned to power for the last time, but the House of Lords defeated or weakened most of his major measures, on the basis that they lacked proven public support. Two further heavy election defeats, in 1895 and 1900, suggested that the Liberals had few answers to the charge of their Conservative and Unionist opponents that they were sectional faddists, while the Unionists upheld empire, national interests, monarchy and institutions.

The pre-war Liberal Party, the constitution and the labour interest

Liberal revival came eventually, between 1902 and 1905, because events allowed them to mount a series of effective and traditional attacks on the Conservatives: on the cost and failures of the Boer War, on the controversial 1902 Education Act and above all on the dramatic proposals by some Conservatives to bring back tariffs (see pages 57–9). The Liberals won a landslide in the 1906 election, when the Conservatives lost 246 of the 402 seats they had won in 1900. They seemed to have regained the centre ground of politics. But the House of Lords rejected their flagship bills, in a successful bid to damage their momentum. Their Education Bill proposed to abolish rate aid to Anglican and Catholic schools and was disliked by Irish MPs as well as many religious parents. Their Licensing Bill aimed to close a third of pubs within 14 years and nationalize the rest; it was rejected by the Lords after a protest of 250,000 people (and 85 brass bands) in Hyde Park. By the time the premiership passed from the dying Henry Campbell-Bannerman to Henry Asquith in April 1908, momentum was draining from the government, which lost seven by-elections in that year. It was badly in need of a reset.

Moreover, Liberal leaders did not think that the strategy of pursuing a reset through a policy of further democratization was likely to work. Forty per cent of the adult male electorate still lacked the vote, because they were not the head of a household (many adult sons lived at home with their father) or because they moved lodgings too frequently to qualify for each year's electoral register. But these people lacked collective identity as an excluded class, had no specific interests that seemed neglected and were of little interest to radicals hoping to find a visible interest group to support. There was no enthusiasm for enfranchising those in receipt of poor relief or otherwise deemed the "unrespectable poor". Liberal enthusiasm for democracy was tempered by the Conservative victories of 1895 and 1900 on a ticket of popular imperialism, and by trade unions' pressure for separate labour representation. Party organizers requested the abolition of "plural voting", the right of those with more than one property to vote in different constituencies at the same election; Liberal agents estimated that this cost the party 30 seats. But even this was problematic, because Conservatives insisted that Ireland's over-representation in the Commons should be addressed at the same time (Pugh 1978).

The idea of male franchise extension was also awkward because of its consequences for the women's suffrage issue. Some Liberals, including John Stuart Mill, had argued for female suffrage in 1866–7, on the grounds that women of education and property were as fit for the vote as their male equivalents, and in the hope of promoting women's other legal rights. In 1907, an Act confirmed the right of women to sit on councils, and several women, all Liberals, became council mayors before 1914. However, after the democratization of 1884, talk of "fitness" for the vote waned. The easiest reform would be to extend the principle of enfranchising heads of household to women who owned property independently, but it was assumed that this would benefit the Conservatives. Periodically the issue was raised in parliament; Conservative MPs sometimes exploited it to embarrass the Liberal leadership. Gladstone and Asquith justified their coolness towards women's enfranchisement by talking about female purity and lack of experience of the political rough-and-tumble, while others talked about unfitness and sentimentality. Such talk appealed particularly to male advocates of "national efficiency", who worried that British party politics was already too populist and undisciplined to address effectively the threat from the militarized continental powers. Most trade unions were also lukewarm about women's suffrage, as were Irish MPs who feared that the accompanying redistribution of seats would reduce their numerical strength. In the years before 1914, the campaign of a minority of militant suffragettes gave Asquith the chance to portray them as law-breakers. The upshot was that no consensus emerged for any solution to the suffrage issue before 1914. Conciliation Bills proposing enfranchisement for women property-owners were introduced between 1910 and 1912 but failed. Backbench Liberal MPs increasingly sympathized with the constitutional suffrage campaign and disliked the lack of legislative progress. A Liberal election victory in 1915 would almost certainly have led to an Act to extend the franchise for women and men. Instead, it fell to Lloyd George's coalition to enfranchise propertied women over 30 and all men over 21 in 1918 (Pugh 1980: 26–29).

The government found a cause instead in the battle against the obstruction practised by the House of Lords. According to one Liberal newspaper, it was becoming the monopoly vested interest behind which all the others – "monopolies in land, in liquor, in ecclesiasticism" – lurked (Bernstein 1986: 123). In 1908–9, Asquith and his new Chancellor David Lloyd George prepared an ambitious budget designed to meet the large costs of new Dreadnought battleships and old age pensions. This required extra taxes on all sections of the community, but Lloyd George emphasized his plans for new land taxes, on the grounds that landowners who collected high rents for valuable land were not contributing enough to society. In a famous speech at Limehouse, he railed against dukes who cost the country as much as two Dreadnoughts. The original aim was simply a propaganda victory over the Lords, on the assumption that they would not reject a budget, which by convention was regarded as a matter for elected representatives in the Commons. However, in November the Conservative majority in the Lords did reject it, arguing that the proposed tax changes were so revolutionary that they required a specific electoral mandate.

This was a major political error. The Liberals responded by proposing to remove the Lords' ability to veto measures proposed by the Commons. The ensuing battle encompassed two bitterly contested and inconclusive general elections in 1910, which left the Liberals in government but dependent on the support of Irish Nationalist and Labour MPs. Both groups had good reason to support the abolition of the Lords' veto. Lloyd George's People's Budget eventually passed, but Tories continued to resist veto abolition, until 1911, by which time Asquith persuaded the new King George V to propose hundreds of new peers if they did not give in. Everyone was aware that the removal of the veto would force the government to reintroduce a Home Rule Bill, which the Liberals had avoided doing during their first term of office. Since the Parliament Act prevented the Lords from vetoing a bill once the Commons had sent it to them for three consecutive sessions, Irish Home Rule dominated the three years after 1911. Meanwhile the budget diminished the appeal of the Conservatives' Tariff Reform proposals, since it reduced the sense of national fiscal crisis. So the Conservatives' decision of November 1909 destroyed their three main policy gambits: their use of the Lords to prevent sectional Liberal measures, their block on Irish self-government and their vision of consolidating British world power around closer imperial ties and external tariffs.

The controversies of 1909–11 made party politics an absorbing spectator sport. At the election of January 1910, turnout was nearly 87 per cent, a record; over the three elections beginning in 1906, it was always over 80 per cent. The battle of the parties was followed by the press as enthusiastically as they followed football and cricket. Politicians, like sportsmen, appeared on cigarette cards. Middle-class girls' schools held mock elections (Sunderland 2020). This was the heyday of the colour election poster; the parties produced millions for the two 1910 elections. They dramatized the issues for popular consumption with wit and some vulgarity. So did newspaper cartoons claiming, for example, that "Tariff Reform means Dog Meat" (Lawrence 2009: 80–82). All this publicity validated the role of parliamentary politics in national life.

Asquith undoubtedly found the management of all these issues very draining. His greatest skill was to manage business neatly and efficiently, but he had to prevaricate endlessly when confronted by what he thought was irrational behaviour by his opponents in these battles. However, this kept the government in control of the agenda, making clear to their Labour and Irish Nationalist supporters that the Liberals would determine what they were offered and when. It is in this context that the Liberal Party's handling of the "labour interest" should be assessed.

Franchise extension in 1867 and 1884 naturally led labour organizations to lobby for their interests to be addressed. The Trades Union Congress was founded in 1868 and unions were recognized as legal entities by Gladstone's government in 1871. But when they organized on a larger scale in the 1880s and 1890s, many employers – and judges – regarded them as a dangerous threat. In 1900, the courts, and the House of Lords, ruled, in the Taff Vale case, that a union was a registered society liable for any damages incurred by employers owing to strike action. Trade unionists and their sympathizers were outraged at this threat to the legitimacy of strikes. It gave an immense impetus to the cause of labour representation in parliament.

The Liberal government made it a priority to respond. In its first session in power, in 1906 a Labour-originated Trades Disputes Act was passed, securing immunity from prosecution for damages incurred in trades disputes. The Lords did not dare to reject it. Further judicial rulings, in 1909–11, labelled the "Osborne Judgment", declared that trade unions could not use subscriptions for political purposes, such as the funding of Labour candidates, unless this was specified in their rules. Again the Liberal government responded, with an Act of 1913 which confirmed that union political funds were lawful, and that individual members must apply to opt out of paying them. It also brought in salaries for MPs in 1911.

So Liberals were determined to remove obstructions to the special status of trade unions. They aimed to show that labour representation in parliament was already able to achieve its legitimate concerns. The Labour Representation Committee (1900) and the Labour Party (1906) had been founded to address the sense of working-class powerlessness during the decade of Tory electoral hegemony after 1895. In 1908, the Miners' Federation decided that their MPs would also sit as Labour men. Labour activists complained that business leaders dominated Liberal Party organization in most industrial towns. The failure of local

Liberals to select more working men as parliamentary candidates forced the Liberal Party chief whip Herbert Gladstone to agree a pact with the Labour Representation Committee's secretary Ramsay MacDonald in 1903, to give each other's party a clear run in over 30 seats. This boosted labour representation: after 1910, there were 42 Labour MPs and 272 Liberal ones.

Liberal legislation signalled an intention to give unions legislative justice, irrespective of any failure of understanding between the parties at constituency level. The Liberals acknowledged the political benefits of working with a small phalanx of Labour MPs in union-dominated constituencies; Labour backing for the Liberals in 1910 clearly strengthened the government's electoral appeal overall (Blewett 1972: 408–9). But it was essential to discourage contests between existing Liberal candidates and Labour ones, which would do both sides harm. Fortunately for the Liberals, Labour made no headway against them in three-cornered contests in 1910, and usually came bottom of the poll. Nor did they cut through in by-elections thereafter (Blewett 1972: 393–4; Clarke 1975). Moreover, despite the Miners' Federation support for Labour, most miner voters continued to prefer Liberals.

An election was due in 1915, although the outbreak of war prevented it. A Plural Voting Bill was near enactment when war broke out; that might well have gained the Liberals 30 seats at the poll. The point of tension would have been the health of the Liberal–Labour electoral pact. The Conservatives had taken between 43 and 46 per cent of the vote in the three 1906 and 1910 elections. If Labour had stood more candidates against Liberals in 1915, splitting the anti-Tory vote, the Liberals would probably have lost (Dutton 2012: 50–1). But given Labour weakness in and since 1910, this would not have been in Labour's short-term interest. In 1912, the Liberal cabinet discussed the idea of introducing the 'alternative vote' (AV) at elections, giving each voter a second-choice vote in three-cornered contests. Had Labour separatism been a major fear, this change would have helped to address it. But the cabinet decided that it was not, that AV would encourage it and that the idea should be abandoned (Pugh 1978: 15–16). It is tantalizing to speculate on how this debate would have been played out in and after a close election in 1915.

The government undoubtedly faced awkward problems in dealing with industrial tensions before the war: 40 million days were lost in strikes in 1912. Unemployment levels were one issue in the first set of by-election defeats for the Liberals in 1907–8. Labour demanded the "right to work" – a bill to require government to provide work or maintenance for the unemployed – and a minimum wage. Both suggestions attracted support from Liberal backbenchers. The government did not tolerate the idea. Instead it offered labour exchanges to facilitate the search for work and a scheme of contributory unemployment insurance for two and a quarter million men in seasonal or cyclical industries, such as building and shipbuilding. Employers, employees and the state would all contribute to the costs of tiding men over their enforced winter inactivity. It also established trade boards to negotiate minimum wages for weakly unionized workers in the "sweated" industries, a principle that it then extended to the strike-plagued coal mines in 1912. Coal miners had also won a statutory eight-hour day in 1908, although unions had already achieved that for most of them. Government thus stuck to the position that it should encourage discussion and arbitration but should remain above the class battle. G. R. Searle has shown that during this period there were few business defections from the Liberal parliamentary party, and that its commercial MPs mostly still saw themselves as progressives pitted against an overprivileged landlord interest (Searle 1983).

Politics after the war turned increasingly on the tensions between capital and labour. It is tempting to assume that in 1912–14 these issues were already dominant, but this was not the case. Many competing issues made up the national political conversation. The Labour Party would undoubtedly have liked to break free from the Liberals in principle, as third parties in such situations generally do, but logic tends to keep them together. It seems likely that an election contest in 1915 would have required the two allies to continue their cooperation against the greater threat posed by the Conservatives. The Liberal government needed to avoid alienating either element of its coalition of middle- and working-class supporters, and its tax policies, discussed in Chapter 2, generally appealed to both. All things considered, it was in a good position to fight an election, in a remarkable turnaround from its history before 1906. In 1914, Liberals could still make the political weather and hold the political centre. For a series of very disabling reasons, after 1918 their two opponents made it instead, and were determined to destroy them.

2

The Liberal state and the liberal world

Most of the confusion in discussing political Liberalism comes from the field of economics. Economists use the term "liberal" to indicate a belief in the efficacy of free markets and the doctrine of "laissez-faire". It is widely assumed, therefore, that Liberalism in politics must be associated with laissez-faire ideas. The many critics of economic "neo-liberalism" since the 1980s have kept that association alive: to them, modern "neoliberalism" is the only liberalism worth discussing. But this is a historically uninformed argument. Very few British political historians now present the Liberal Party at any time as a laissez-faire body. Liberalism was a political movement that had to respond to public grievances about existing conditions, including economic conditions, and these often required state action.

This is not to deny that there were rigid laissez-faire economists in the Liberal Party, some of whom were influential. In the nineteenth century, one strand of opinion urged low state spending and taxation at all costs. The behaviour of the leading elite politicians in this camp is suggestive. Lord Lansdowne in the late 1820s, Charles Wood in the 1840s, Robert Lowe in the 1860s and George Goschen in the 1880s all advocated cooperation with the Conservatives at important moments to safeguard principles of economy and laissez-faire. They did so because they disliked the alternative policy that many Liberals were advocating, which, at most of these times, was parliamentary reform. They feared that Reform would introduce uncontrollable pressures for unattractive policies, and specifically for more state intervention and spending. Their camp always lost the argument. Lowe, Goschen and Lansdowne's grandson (the fifth Marquess) were high-profile defectors from the party in 1886, in opposition to Gladstone's policy of Irish Home Rule but also to democratic politics after 1885.

Nineteenth-century Liberals were committed to the idea of keeping taxes low, allowing trade to flourish across the globe and checking extravagance in government. They believed that this would not only help the economy but also bolster state authority by defusing radical attacks. Since the late eighteenth century, radicals, stimulated by British republican ideas and the French Revolution, had taken up the cry of "old corruption". They argued that the political elite must be purged because it abused its position to seize taxpayers' money for its own purposes. Between 1815 and the 1870s, governments of both parties succeeded in blunting and neutralizing this critique, by modest institutional reform and by tax and tariff reductions. This made the state look comparatively "disinterested": free from vested interest control. Purifying the state of the excesses of old corruption did as much to legitimize its authority as parliamentary reform did.

These modest reforms also aimed to justify remaining government spending, most of which went on foreign and defence policy. Some radicals demanded economy at home and non-intervention abroad. Palmerston led the process of creating a counter-narrative: that targeted intervention helped Britain to keep itself safe and to promote global liberalism. His views were particularly dominant in the 1850s, but it remained true, throughout the century, that the Liberal Party never spoke with just one voice on foreign affairs.

The 1867 Reform Act was a major watershed in domestic politics because the arrival of "democracy" in the towns destroyed the underpinnings of traditional "old corruption" language. It seemed hardly plausible that a selfish elite still controlled the state. The Gladstonian Liberal Party aimed to show that "the people" could now shape the political sphere, under Liberal guidance. Gladstone's popular speeches still emphasized the importance of economy, because he was one of the last still to worry about combatting the old radical allegations. In time, however, the Liberal Party naturally became the home of those who demanded more spending on social issues and an attack on antisocial monopolies. In particular, the institutions of the Poor Law became a major concern, once many voters worried that they might need to use them. Meanwhile, as the world became a more challenging place after 1880, the cost of defence to maintain peace and free trade grew dramatically.

The primary political question became, not the principle of intervention at home or abroad, but who should pay for domestic and defence spending. Insofar as there was a "New Liberalism" before 1914, it was not a new ideology proposing a revised relationship between the state and the citizen. It was a successful rebranding exercise designed to show the electorate that the Liberal Party had the fairest and most efficient tax policy to meet the costs of liberal politics.

Peace, retrenchment and "old corruption"

"Peace, retrenchment and reform" was a favoured slogan of early nineteenth-century reformers. Indeed it was periodically taken up by later Liberal leaders to show their fidelity to party traditions: by Gladstone in the Midlothian campaign of 1879–80 and by the Liberal leader Henry Campbell-Bannerman in 1905. In the 1820s, Whigs and radicals paid as much attention to "peace" and "retrenchment" as they did to "reform". The two main charges on the taxpayer were defence spending and the debt incurred to pay for the French wars. The third was the cost of government posts. In every economic depression between 1780 and 1850, hard-pressed taxpayers demanded the abolition of unnecessary offices, the reduction of public salaries and a scaling back of overseas military commitments.

Radical reformers took these taxpayer complaints further and turned them into an overarching critique of the political elite. They asserted that politics was a system of "old corruption", a conspiracy by small numbers of well-connected people. They said that ministers sought government office to control the levers of political patronage and keep themselves in power. They could then feather the nests of friends and relations by offering them well-paid sinecures, or give salaried posts to potential supporters in return for their vote. After the Napoleonic Wars, radicals compiled long lists of unnecessary official posts and their costs, most famously John Wade's *Black Book* of 1820 (Harling 1996: 143–8). Cartoonists lampooned the extravagance and gluttony of George IV, as a symbol of the greed and selfishness of a monstrously overweight political regime.

After the French wars ended in 1815, Lord Liverpool's Tory government (1812–27) was very aware of taxpayer and merchant grievances about government spending. It abolished thousands of public offices, abandoned the property tax in 1816, relinquished its patronage powers over customs posts in 1821 and reduced tariffs in the 1820s. This "liberal" policy undoubtedly benefited its public standing. Since 1780, the opposition had regularly brought a motion to parliament that the "influence of the Crown" (through patronage politics) was too great. It abandoned it after 1822, in an acknowledgement that the government had greatly reduced its manipulation of patronage to shore up its parliamentary position.

However, calls for retrenchment resurfaced in the severe depression of 1829–30. The Reform government responded not just by abolishing nomination boroughs but by renewed zeal for economy. In 1835, public expenditure reached a low for the century, helped by a very cautious foreign policy. Diplomatic service spending was moved from the civil list and put under parliamentary control. After a wave of further sinecure abolitions in 1831–2, a Select Committee of 1834 could find hardly any remaining. A Royal Commission of 1832 inaugurated a similar policy of office and salary reduction in the Church of England. Meanwhile the 1834 Poor Law reduced the burden of the poor rate (Harling 1996: 208–16).

Most elite Whigs and Liberals did not want to take this retrenchment policy as far as radicals. As noted in Chapter 1, they believed in the principle of "good government" across the country, particularly in areas of education, public health and law reform. The activist social policy of the 1830s and 1840s required new forms of patronage: the reforms of the Poor Law, prisons, schools and factory conditions all involved the appointment of inspectors and other civil servants to ensure their implementation. Whig families assumed that upbringing in the right political principles helped to guarantee public-spirited behaviour, so they had no problem with the idea of patronage. Opportunities to rise through examinations, or retire with pensions, were very rare; almost everyone relied on connections to advance their careers and secure an income. In 1831, Prime Minister Grey secured offices for his family retinue worth £60,000 a year, even as his government introduced sweeping parliamentary reform (Knights 2021: 411–13). In 1846, Prime Minister Russell gave the historian-politician Macaulay the post of Paymaster General, to give him "leisure and quiet" to continue his *History of England* (Parry 1996: 146). By the 1841 election, Melbourne's government was running big deficits, contributing to its defeat. This was mainly because of the severe economic situation, to some degree because of its social reforms, and because Foreign Secretary Palmerston required more ships to meet the international challenges of 1838–40.

Meanwhile the severe economic depression of 1838–42 unleashed major protests, in the form of Chartism and demands for the repeal of import tariffs on corn to lower the price of bread. The Conservative government of Sir Robert Peel (1841–6) intensified the Liberal Tory policy of the 1820s, aiming to reduce tax burdens on consumers and businesses and to improve the efficiency of government. Peel's approach focused on reductions in indirect taxes and on restricting expenditure on foreign and defence policy. Peel was a more committed political economist than most Liberals, indeed a rigid advocate of free market principles.

Peel's repeal of the Corn Laws in 1846 did more than anything to show that the state was not biased in favour of a "landed interest". It also prompted a Conservative backbench revolt which ended his government and left his main disciples, Sir James Graham and William Gladstone, politically homeless. Gladstone moved into the Liberal Party in the 1850s, because he had convinced himself that he could make it a zealous force for tax-cutting and more efficient government. Gladstone disliked the lax spending policies of Palmerston's 1855–8 government, but this made him all the more convinced of the opportunity for a Peelite policy of retrenchment, financial equilibrium and "resistance to abuses"; he made himself its champion (Shannon 2007: 107).

For Gladstone, this was a way to show sympathy with radicals' economic instincts in order to spike their political intentions. Between 1847 and 1850, with the continent in turmoil and both main parties in disarray at home, radical MPs launched a series of demands for institutional reform. In 1848, a Financial Reform Association was founded in Liverpool, urging an end to all indirect taxes, and attacking extravagance, the pension list, and army and aristocratic "drones" (Calkins 1960). The leader of this radical movement was Richard Cobden, the son of an impoverished Sussex yeoman farmer. Cobden had become famous as the main spokesman for the Anti-Corn Law League. After 1846, he continued his attack on the landed interest and on state spending. His vision for the globe was that small-scale industrial and agricultural producers would trade harmoniously with each other across the seas, having dismantled the feudal, aristocratic, militarist and bureaucratic systems that imposed tariffs and high taxes for their own benefit (Cain 1979). In 1849, Cobden proposed a 10 per cent salary cut for higher officials.

Gladstone found his political vocation in late 1852, when he was made Chancellor of the Exchequer in Lord Aberdeen's Peelite–Liberal coalition government. He turned the 1853 budget into a major exercise to show the disinterestedness, yet dynamism, of the state. He continued this strategy as chancellor throughout Palmerston's Liberal government of 1859–65. His budgets of 1853 and 1860 reduced the number of articles liable to customs duty from 466 to 48, of which only 15 were of significance; none were on raw materials, raw foodstuffs or manufactured goods. Between 1860 and 1865, income tax fell from 10d to 4d, and tea duties were reduced by two-thirds. Gladstone also promoted what later became called "Treasury control" over other departments' spending. Charles Trevelyan, the Treasury's chief civil servant from 1840 to 1859, was an even greater advocate of this, having initially made his reputation in India, aged 22, with a campaign against East India Company officials who took gifts. A Committee of Public Accounts was created in 1861. In 1853, Gladstone commissioned an investigation into civil service organization, leading to the Northcote–Trevelyan Report of 1854. At this point, the Peelite Gladstone saw administrative reform as a better way of stabilizing and purifying the state than another Reform Bill (Parry 1993: 183–6).

By the 1850s, radicals were concentrating their demands for retrenchment on defence spending. Cobden's most distinctive campaign after 1846, in company with fellow radical John Bright, was for an international peace movement. They presented diplomatic activity and high defence costs as frauds on the public which gave an illusory sense of protection while increasing the risk of war. In 1850, Cobden used the Select Committee on Official Salaries to propose sweeping reductions in diplomatic representation and remuneration. In 1854, they opposed the Crimean War.

Liberal intervention in Europe

Liberal tensions over foreign policy and defence spending were encapsulated by the long-running verbal warfare between Cobden and the Liberals' main foreign policy spokesman, Viscount Palmerston. Palmerston was foreign secretary in every Liberal government between 1830 and 1852, and prime minister from 1855 to 1858 and from 1859 until his death in 1865. He had joined the government of 1830 as one of the leading members of a "Liberal Tory" faction. The word "liberal" had entered British politics in the 1810s and 1820s in the context of the debates about Spanish liberals' battle for constitutional reform and Irish Catholics' campaign for seats in the United Kingdom Parliament. It implied a commitment to civil and religious liberties everywhere (in contrast to stagnant and exclusive aristocratic and clerical Toryism) as well as a willingness to listen to popular grievances about taxation and to communicate government policy better to the public.

Palmerston was a vigorous administrator, not a radical reformer. He supported Reform in 1830 to give government more confidence and legitimacy. He applied the same principle to foreign policy: he wanted to engage parliamentary and public interest in foreign and defence issues, so as to educate penny-pinching British taxpayers that, while economy was good, swift intervention abroad was also sometimes necessary (Parry 2006: 150–51). He argued that Britain needed to spend money maintaining its global naval predominance, so that the world's seas remained open for British merchants. British trade could then naturally expand into South America, the Ottoman Empire and China. He upheld keenly the navy's decades-long campaign against the international slave trade and its defence of Canada, which seemed threatened by the United States.

Palmerston was particularly anxious to assert Britain's right and duty to intervene periodically in European affairs. Here he followed his mentors Canning and Pitt. The narrowness of the English Channel meant that Britain could not wisely ignore European politics. No power or consortium of powers, whether led by France, Austria or Russia, must be allowed to dominate the continent. More particularly, France must be prevented from expanding eastwards towards the Scheldt and the Rhine, thus facilitating an invasion of Britain. But French revisionism was not Britain's only concern in Europe. In 1814–15, Russia, Austria and Prussia established the mechanism of the Concert of Europe to discuss diplomatic tensions. They hoped that cooperation of this sort between the European powers would check any revived French ambitions, but their idea of the Concert was also ideological: they wanted the powers to suppress liberal and national movements on the continent and the instability that they might trigger.

Led by Grey and Palmerston, the governments of the 1830s developed a strategy of dealing with this double threat, by working with France, over Belgium, Spain and Portugal, to restrain its ambitions while excluding the eastern powers from the action. The hope was to teach France that it would benefit by cooperating with Britain. The two countries recognized the independence of Belgium, once that part of the old Kingdom of the Netherlands rebelled against it in 1830. They also cooperated throughout the 1830s to support the constitutionalists in the civil wars in Spain and Portugal. In neither arena were the eastern powers able to develop an alternative policy. Iberia and the Low Countries were the places where British troops had been most active in the French wars. Keeping up British influence there in cooperation with France would prevent France getting sole control of key ports that would directly threaten British interests.

The informal Anglo-French understanding established by Liberal governments in the 1830s has remained, despite challenges, the basis of British foreign policy for 200 years. By working together to defend constitutionalism in Belgium, Iberia and later Italy, the two countries created an idea of "the West". Palmerston established the unwritten principle of British foreign policy that France was a more reliable ally than any other great power, as long as it accepted the British worldview about the benefits of peace and stability, rather than a Napoleonic thirst for revenge. French support became a significant boost to British diplomatic clout in Europe, but this also meant that at times of French uncooperativeness or weakness, Britain struggled to have much weight. In the 1830s, both countries were liberal constitutional monarchies; their parliaments were dominated by commercial interests hostile to high spending and to war. The 1830 Revolution in France, like Britain's change of government that year, seemed to demonstrate that respectable public opinion was now a beneficent force that could be marshalled for the promotion of constitutional progress.

The understanding remained informal, because representative politicians in both countries could not resist sometimes trading insults for electoral benefit. Palmerston was not above making fun of the French himself, but he remained a firm supporter of the entente and lost office in 1851 and 1858 as a result. France remained a major naval rival, and some of its politicians naturally wished to reassert its once dominant place in Europe. Napoleon Bonaparte's long war on Britain loomed very large in the British popular imagination; he remained a demonic figure to many. When his nephew declared himself Napoleon III in 1852, there was a media panic. In fact, there were three invasion scares between 1845 and 1860, caused not just by French rhetoric but also by technological innovation. The development of steam and then ironclad ships seemed to call Britain's naval superiority into question. Military men argued that Britain must invest in new ships to avoid a cross-Channel invasion. They blamed inadequate defence spending on "Manchesterism", the naïve tax-cutting peace agenda of Cobdenite radicals who were often known as the "Manchester School" (Parry 2001; Partridge 1989).

The invasion scares, and the Crimean War of 1854–6, helped to reawaken national interest in military matters. In 1860, Palmerston's government decisively increased naval spending to adjust to the iron-clad shipping revolution, and Napoleon III never challenged British global maritime supremacy again. But the two countries also agreed a major commercial treaty, negotiated by Cobden, which significantly lowered French tariffs and seemed to pave the way for a freeing of trade throughout the developed world. Several other countries followed suit in the mid-1860s. It seemed that even Napoleon III was acknowledging the benefits of British tutelage.

British support for Italian liberalism after 1848 was another building block of Palmerston's popularity. In the 1850s, Russo-Austrian power in Italy declined, allowing an independent Italian constitutional monarchy to emerge in 1860–61 under Piedmont's leadership. British diplomacy claimed much of the credit. In October 1860, Russell, now Palmerston's foreign secretary, publicly praised the Italians for building up their liberties, insisted that the public opinion of Europe was with them and warned the powers not to interfere (Russell 1870: II, 282). Any pretence of British respect for a "Concert" had disappeared. In 1864, the Italian freedom fighter Garibaldi enjoyed a brief but triumphant progress through Britain.

International historians who admire nineteenth-century Concert diplomacy for its stabilizing effects have little time for Palmerston (Schroeder 1994). In western Europe, he thought that the Concert was a ploy to repress legitimate and beneficial constitutional movements.

From the late 1840s, Anglo-French cooperation also weakened it in the east, where Britain had earlier found it more useful. Britain and France now worked to undermine Russian support for the Ottoman sultan, and to encourage him instead to give more civil rights to his Christian subjects, in return for the protection of western Europe. The result was the Crimean War of 1854–56, in which Britain and France fought with the Ottomans against Russia. In 1856, Anglo-French pressure led to an international guarantee to preserve the independence and integrity of the Ottoman Empire, in return for which the sultan promised equal legal and civil rights for Christians, which British liberals hoped would stabilize the Balkans. Western capital, mainly from Britain and France, now poured into Ottoman lands, attracted by high interest rates. Britain and France cooperated in several other parts of the world after 1856, especially in opening up China to Western commerce. Their gung-ho approach to extending Western values through Asia now seems assertively imperialist, although it did not involve any major territorial acquisitions.

Liberalism, the state and the demise of "old corruption"

After Palmerston's death and the passage of a major Reform Act in 1867, many people expected that radicals would dominate the Liberal agenda, leading to an assault on elitist institutions at home and on military spending abroad. At the 1868 election, it was common to point to Cobden's plans of 1848–9 to reduce central state expenditure by £10 million back to the 1835 level (whereas in fact £10 million had been added during the Palmerstonian era, to make £70 million in all). Some radicals, such as Joseph Chamberlain and Charles Dilke, now looked to the United States as the best model for English-speaking peoples: it had no Church Establishment or monarchy and a much smaller diplomatic service. Radical MPs criticized the cost and utility of the monarchy, especially in the light of Queen Victoria's invisibility after Albert's death and the Prince of Wales's involvement in a high-profile divorce case. In 1871, 51 MPs voted to reduce the allowance that parliament was asked to give her son Arthur.

Gladstone, who became prime minister after the 1868 election, shared these financial objectives but not the broader political ones. His aim was still to fight the battle against "old corruption" by continually demonstrating the fairness and neutrality of the state. At the election, he attacked the minority Conservative government's increased spending on the military establishment and other "knots and groups, and I may say classes". He claimed that this "Continental system of feeding the desires of classes and portions of the community at the expense of the whole" was directly related to the Conservatives' absence of a popular mandate (Parry 2018: 15).

Gladstone's determination to show that the liberal state had transcended vested interest politics was shown in the introduction of competitive examinations across almost the whole civil service in 1870, removing the Treasury's vestigial remaining patronage powers. His government also reduced defence expenditure from £27.1 million to £21.1 million between 1867–8 and 1869–70, particularly by requiring the self-governing British colonies to spend more on self-defence. It boldly asserted its control over the military administration. The Horse Guards, the seat of the power of the Duke of Cambridge, the royal commander-in-chief, was moved to Pall Mall and placed under the control of a cabinet minister. Reform of the promotion system in the army in 1871 aimed to instil more professionalism in the elite officer class.

The assertive radical campaign against state institutions quickly lost momentum. The introduction of the principle of household franchise in 1867 undermined the old radical view that the state was institutionally corrupt. Cobden had died in 1865, but the veteran radical John Bright entered the cabinet in December 1868, telling his constituents that the time had come when an honest man might enter the service of the Crown and yet not feel it necessary to "dissociate himself from his own people" (Trevelyan 1914: 398).

Foreign difficulties helped to undermine pressure for further spending and tax cuts. In 1870–71, the Franco-Prussian war and the unification of Germany showed that the world had become a more uncertain place and led to another invasion scare and defence panic. The defence spending cuts of 1868–70 were reversed, and from now on Gladstone failed to rally the party in favour of further reductions. His call to abolish income tax at the 1874 election was a damp squib. His acceptance of international arbitration of the Alabama Claims, a Civil War-era dispute with the United States, backfired in 1872 when the press found the costly settlement humiliating. Radicals increasingly abandoned the Cobdenite cry that high foreign and defence policy expenditure was merely a way of subsidizing lazy aristocrats. Instead, in the 1880s radical leaders Chamberlain and Dilke advocated a vigorous defence of British interests abroad, identifying the commercial benefits of this approach and complaining at the effeteness of the Foreign Office for failing to adopt it. Frequent imperial wars and international disputes in the 1870s and 1880s also transformed the political standing of the army, which benefited from unprecedented, excited and patriotic newspaper coverage of the campaigns (Parry 2006: 291–3, 365–8).

Continuing radical attacks on institutions – such as the criticisms of the royal family made by Dilke and G. O. Trevelyan in 1871–2 – were exploited by the Conservative opposition. Disraeli's high-profile attack on the Gladstone government in 1872 was founded on the claim that an unpatriotic Liberal radicalism was "assail[ing] or menac[ing] every institution and every interest" (Parry 2011: 179). At the general election of 1874, and again in 1885, the Conservatives were the beneficiaries – and stokers – of a "Church in danger" furore. The Conservative revival in London in 1874 was boosted by the meddling of Gladstone's Endowed Schools Commission with established local and religious middle-class schools (see page 74). One of Disraeli's first acts as prime minister in 1874, significantly, was to abolish the Commission (Goldman 2006).

Overall state expenditure in 1885 was 32 per cent higher than in 1867, after two full terms of Gladstonian Liberal government; income tax was 8d in 1885 against the 6d bequeathed by Disraeli in 1880. The monarchy, the army and the Church survived not because they had been significantly reformed but because radicalism lost its edge. Queen Victoria and the Duke of Cambridge continued to influence foreign and military policy. Continuing Treasury accusations of army jobbery reflected its inability to rein in the military men. The Foreign Office continued to evade pressure for cuts in the diplomatic service (Parry 2011: 184).

The Liberal Party itself quickly accepted that the debate had moved on from "old corruption" and "disinterestedness" and that state action could be beneficial on public utility grounds. Chamberlain claimed in 1885 that a government chosen by the people should have more power than former regimes controlled by a small class. In 1883, the Liberal MP G. W. E. Russell (Lord John's nephew) asserted that modern

Liberalism defined the state as the embodiment of the nation, and "the one sovereign agent for all moral, material, and social reforms" (Russell 1883: 925).

Gladstone's 1868 government continued the theme of the 1830s governments: that the state had a duty to improve prospects for the people while also trying to shape their character. Its most important legislation was the 1870 Elementary Education Act, which finally established a national system of schools, by setting up ratepayer-funded school boards to build and maintain them where the existing provision by religious and philanthropic bodies was deemed inadequate by inspectors. In October 1867, Edward Miall, formerly a leader of Nonconformist voluntaryism (see page 69), signalled his change of mind to support government interference in education, arguing that after franchise extension the old grounds for popular suspicion of it had disappeared (Miall 1884: 273). The 1880 Liberal government brought in compulsory education and in 1882 laid down a broader curriculum, which the state subsidized. Between 1870 and 1885, government spending on education rose threefold.

As it had done after 1832, government after 1867 took advantage of its increased legitimacy to discipline working-class behaviour more assertively. There was a renewed campaign against perceived over-generosity in the provision of Poor Law relief. More stringent sanctions were applied against fathers of illegitimate children. Pubs were required to abide by compulsory opening hours and penalties for drunkenness were increased. Twice-convicted criminals were placed under supervision for seven years after discharge (Parry 1993: 240–41).

One of the favourite principles of laissez-faire economists was that the state should not interfere with "free contracts" made between employers and adult workmen. Yet Liberal governments had already recognized how exploitative these could be, when men had little choice of work. Russell's government was the first to limit hours of adult work in factories, in the Ten Hours legislation of 1847 and 1850, in response to the revelations of Royal Commissions on conditions of work in mines and factories. In the 1880s, Gladstone's government passed two pieces of legislation protecting rural tenants from the operation of freedom of contract principles, the Ground Game Act of 1880 and the Agricultural Holdings Act of 1883. Liberal land reform in Ireland and Scotland involved greater incursions of those principles, which were justified with reference to the alternative forms of landholding that had historically taken root there (Dewey 1974; Parry 1993: 243–5, 293–4).

In 1880, the Oxford academic T. H. Green gave a lecture criticizing freedom of contract principles. This is sometimes portrayed as a searing critique of classical Liberalism, but he was merely defending Gladstone's legislation. Indeed he argued that for 50 years the Liberals had been fighting "the same old cause of social good against class interests" (Richter 1964: 283–6). In 1885, Arthur Elliot and G. O. Trevelyan both maintained that it had been standard Liberal doctrine since the debates over slavery and the Irish Church in the 1830s that parliament could interfere with private property subject to compensation, and that all public endowments were public property subject to public inquiry (Parry 2006: 83).

Most government intervention was done at local level, where the principle of democratic involvement was crucial in legitimizing it, as Chapter 3 discusses further. Most early expansion of social provision was done through permissive legislation. In 1906, for example, an Act of the new Liberal government allowed local education authorities to provide free school meals (charging them either to parents or the rates). It derived from a suggestion from the Bradford authority which had been providing them, and from the local Labour MP and two women campaigners.

Democratic pressure had most effect on the debate about the Poor Laws. Many working- and middle-class people depended on efficient Poor Law hospitals. The smallpox epidemics of the early 1880s triggered an important Act of 1883, under which London's hospitals were declared to be sanitary institutions for society as a whole, separate from the Poor Law and its stigma. Most Poor Law authorities became more flexible in their handling of short-term unemployment and used out-relief more than the workhouse. This trend intensified after the Liberal government of 1894 democratized the franchise for electing boards of guardians (which had previously been weighted towards richer ratepayers). Boards were now accountable to electors who might themselves fear occasional unemployment. The amount per head spent on individual paupers doubled between 1870 and 1905, and the cost of the Poor Law tripled. This led to a major debate about the funding of poverty and old age. Ratepayers started to ask why the cost should fall on them rather than the central state (Harris 1983: 72–6).

This increase in the expectations of local and central authorities was a natural process, but it raised awkward questions of funding and taxation. Alarming developments in foreign and defence policy raised these same questions even more acutely.

Liberal defensiveness abroad

Palmerston had pursued a foreign policy that could be presented as explicitly liberal. After 1870, this became increasingly difficult. The Liberal Party no longer found that foreign and imperial policy offered much cause for celebration. Instead Liberals found themselves vulnerable to criticism from Tories and militarists that they should spend more on national interests.

Palmerston's world, in which an Anglo-French entente used naval power to promote constitutional progress in seaboard states against inflexible eastern autocracies, was disappearing. The outbreak of the Franco-Prussian war, the defeat of France, and the unification of Germany profoundly altered the rhythms of European diplomacy. Germany wanted new alliance patterns to suit its own interests. It also had a peacetime army of half a million men. Relations between the armed continental powers became central to diplomacy. Meanwhile the Concert reasserted itself in the east, and most Balkan Christians were given practical independence from the Ottomans at the Congress of Berlin in 1878. This effectively marked the end of the Anglo-French project of the 1840s and 1850s to press the Ottomans to reform their governance.

In the 1880s, a crisis in Egypt revealed how the dynamic of Britain's international relations had changed in ways that Liberals found difficult to negotiate. The potential need to defend Britain's route to India made influence over the Egyptian regime in Cairo essential. Loan arrangements with Western capitalists had driven the Egyptian government to bankruptcy, and Britain and France intervened jointly in 1878 to impose a policy of financial austerity. This created severe unrest, and in 1882 Britain mooted a military intervention to restore order. This might also have been a joint affair, but when the French government demurred, Britain bombarded Alexandria and invaded Egypt on its own. It cited the importance of maintaining law, order and open trade, but its main concern was to ensure that no other power supplanted British influence. Gladstone claimed that the occupation was temporary, on behalf of a European Concert charged with the stability of Ottoman realms – a remnant of his early career Toryism. Those who viewed his claim sceptically were proved right: British troops did not leave Egypt until 1956.

Britain's occupation of Egypt marked the point when its European and imperial needs fused, with the imperial predominating. The occupation alienated both the Ottomans and France. It led Britain to establish an East African security zone for the defence of India that eventually included Sudan, Somaliland, and the lands to the south. It triggered the "Scramble for Africa" among the European powers, which did so much to heighten imperial tensions, and posed particular problems of peacekeeping in southern Africa. In the public imagination, Europe, Africa and India now merged into a vast imperial space. Newspapers suggested that Britain's main duty was the defence of its empire against European rivals; a potentially costly business. The Conservative Party harnessed popular imperialism to attack Liberal half-heartedness in Egypt, Sudan and South Africa.

The Egyptian crisis also had ramifications for the balance of power in Europe. It gave France and Russia a clear reason to cooperate navally against Britain in the Mediterranean, as well as against an increasingly powerful Germany. In 1887, Lord Salisbury's Conservative government made Mediterranean agreements with Italy and Austria, aimed particularly against Russian meddling in the Balkans. The tensions of the mid-1880s created a defence panic in Britain that prompted the Conservatives' 1889 Naval Defence Act, which pledged Britain to keep its navy at the strength of the next two powers put together: France and Russia. This was something that had not been necessary while Palmerston's French entente aimed to keep those two powers at odds. In response, France and Russia negotiated a defence treaty in stages between 1891 and 1894. In 1898, France nearly went to war with Britain over Sudan. It took until 1904 for Britain and France to resolve the tensions created over Egypt, with an entente that secured British predominance in East Africa in return for recognizing France's sphere in Morocco.

The Naval Defence Act was the result of lobbying by the defence establishment and Conservative backbenchers. It was a great political trap for the Liberal Party. In view of the tensions between the European powers, it meant a built-in expansion of expenditure. It was a product of severe anxiety in naval and military circles about the soundness of democratic politics after franchise reform. Yet economizers were now placed permanently on the defensive, because the press took on an increasingly imperialist tone. Together, the Act and the swagger of the media destroyed Gladstone's last premiership. He resigned as prime minister for the final time in early 1894 because he could not accept the Admiralty's increased spending estimates (Keeling 2018). Naval spending rose from £10.2 million in 1880 to £17.5 million in 1895.

Liberals were badly divided on foreign and imperial policy between 1895 and 1905: a faction of Liberal Imperialists tried to counter the Conservatives' charge that the party was inherently unpatriotic. But the Conservatives led Britain into the Boer War between 1899 and 1902, at a cost of £210 million. Meanwhile, from 1898, Germany began to expand its navy. The war made clear that the cost of maintaining Britain's worldwide empire against all rivals was unsustainable. A major debate about British global strategy and defence funding was inevitable. In an attempt to rein in costs, Conservative Foreign Secretary Lord Lansdowne made pacts with Japan, and informally with the United States, as well as with France. Meanwhile Joseph Chamberlain, the ex-Liberal colonial secretary and intellectual powerhouse of the Unionist government, caused a sensation in 1903 when he proposed raising a new funding stream by reintroducing tariffs and a system of imperial preference for industrial goods.

Funding the changed political world

Chamberlain's Tariff Reform proposal aimed to boost British (and imperial) tax revenues. This would fund not only imperial defence but also a new politics based on addressing British social needs. The Boer War had prompted prolonged discussion about improving "national efficiency", after one-third of recruits were found unfit for service (Searle 1971). If 500,000 British soldiers struggled to beat 100,000 Boer farmers, how would the army fare against German military might? Education spending at central and local level was one priority. Chamberlain added centrally funded old age pensions: this was an eye-catching way of reducing the burden placed by the aged on the local Poor Law, and increasing the dignity of voters who feared penury and the workhouse after a lifetime of work. Many Tories had felt since the 1870s that central government must subsidize ratepayers, who had been left to fund the ever-expanding spending on education and the poor. Under pressure from farmers, the Conservatives had remitted half the rates on agricultural land in 1896, but a Royal Commission established in the same year could not agree on a new funding model for local government (Offer 1981: 207–17).

Liberals responded to this debate, first, by defending free trade as better than tariffs for the economy and class relations. Between 1903 and 1906, the Liberal Party united and mobilized with great moral power behind this historic rallying cry. The result was a landslide at the 1906 election, when they won 397 seats, gaining 214 over 1900. At many meetings, they signalled the effect of regressive Conservative food taxes on working-class living standards by presenting two loaves, the Big Free Trade Loaf and the Small Protectionist Loaf, and inquiring which the audience wanted. Election posters asked whether voters were willing to return to the Hungry Forties and the domination of big landed and corporate interests: "Tariff Reform means Trusts for the Rich, Crusts for the Poor" (Trentmann 2008: plates IV, IX).

Coupling free trade with the case for social reform was all very well, but it raised the question of who should pay for it. Most Liberals argued that in principle the landowner should pay more. Some still defined themselves against the monopolizing rural "landed interest", which Cobden had attacked in the 1840s, hence the legislation of the 1880s to protect the rights of tenant farmers in England and crofters in Scotland. But criticism increasingly focused on the urban landlord, whose property was increasing in value because of the dynamism of the urban economy and workforce, not his own capital investment. Therefore surely he should pay something towards the services that kept the urban economy going. As far back as 1871, Goschen had proposed forcing owners and occupiers each to pay a share of local rates, rather than to allow the owner to pass the whole cost to the occupier in increased rent (Offer 1981: 177–80). Many Liberals liked the arguments of the American campaigner Henry George, that high rents reduced the money available for labour and capital, and that taxation of the site value of land would pump surplus rent into the economy to more productive ends. This, however, would require values to be independently ascertained and registered. In practice, the major Liberal land tax reform before 1906 was the introduction of estate duty, a tax on the capital value of land at death, by William Harcourt in his 1894 budget.

The battle for free trade in 1906 allowed the Liberals to revive but also modernize Cobden's agenda of free markets, international peace and anti-landlordism, adding a critique of shady protectionist businesses as well. This was a classic political rebranding, deftly weaving together the old and the new, the practical and the idealistic. It was a revival of "Manchesterism" that, as Tony Howe has pointed out, wrong-footed Cobdenism's philosophical critics (Howe 1997: 227). In 1893–5, a small group of intellectuals had founded the Rainbow Circle to steer the direction of Liberal government policy away from "Manchesterism". In November 1895, Herbert Samuel read the Circle a paper unveiling what he called the "New Liberalism". It was a critique of materialist economics and a declaration that, because of changes in state capacity, modern politics could fuse ethics with economics and create a higher social unity (Freeden 1989: 27–8). Samuel was frustrated by, and overreacting to, the continuing influence of Gladstonian retrenchment policy at that moment. He seemed unaware that Liberals had often used legislation to try to shape character. By 1906, the party had re-emphasized its traditional synthesis of economic and ethical purpose, but, as always, this would continue to evolve. The Rainbow Circle's "New Liberals" contributed usefully to taxation discussions after 1909, because J. A. Hobson's argument about artificial national underconsumption (see page 90) could be used to square the principle of free markets with Lloyd George's personal instincts to tax "the rich" more heavily.

In response to Chamberlain's intervention, the new Liberal government itself adopted the policy of non-contributory old age pensions. In 1907, Asquith, as Chancellor of the Exchequer, announced that they would be funded through the principle of differentiated taxation. Earned income (under £2,000 per year) would be taxed at a lower rate (9d) than unearned and higher income, which would carry on paying the standard rate of 1s. Estate duty was also raised. In other words, differentiation favoured the lower class of taxpayers, who would benefit from retrenchment and peaceful Liberal foreign policy. Foreign Secretary Edward Grey continued Lansdowne's ententes with an agreement with Russia in 1907 (following its damaging defeat by Japan in 1905). Spending on the army and navy fell by 10 per cent between

1905 and 1907. Asquith's Liberalism seemed to offer free trade, peace and retrenchment as well as old age pensions. These were introduced in 1908, at a rate of 5s per week to citizens over 70 who qualified on income grounds.

It is not clear how far Liberal financial radicalism would have developed, had the Germans not begun a new naval building race in 1908. The media and the Admiralty demanded more Dreadnoughts to counter them. Meanwhile the cost of old age pensions had been underestimated: by 1914 the cost was double Asquith's estimate (Searle 2004: 392). By the time of the 1909 budget, the estimated deficit was £16 million. It was politically essential to show that the sum could be raised without resorting to tariffs.

Lloyd George's famous budget of 1909, his first as chancellor, made headlines by embracing the principles of differentiation and graduation and focusing heavily on the rich. It kept tax rates where they were for earned income below £3,000 (that is, at 9d for incomes up to £2,000 and 1s for those between £2,000 and £3,000) but increased the standard rate for those above £3,000 from 1s to 1s2d. It also brought in a super tax of 6d on incomes over £5,000 (on the amounts exceeding £3,000) and higher death duties on estates over £1 million. There was no risk of electoral backlash, as the numbers involved were small: there were only 25,000 taxpayers with incomes of over £3,000. In fact, only one million people paid income tax at all, so the increased duties on spirits and tobacco, which aimed to raise £3.5 million, hit many more voters (Murray 1980). Lloyd George also announced plans for a land valuation scheme in preparation for a future land tax aimed at subsiding the rates. His budget speech focused its attack on the class of greedy and antisocial urban landlords, who benefited from the increased demand for town land but spent as little as possible on improvements, crowded their tenants in unhealthy conditions and lacked any responsible personal relationship with them (Hansard 29 April 1909: 532–7).

When it was necessary to raise more money in the 1914 budget, partly because of the cost of pensions but mostly because of the increased naval threat from Germany, this same policy was extended. Death duties were raised on estates worth over £60,000, and incomes over £2,500 were taxed more highly, through an extension of the super tax and of the principle of income tax graduation.

So the main consequence of Lloyd George's budgets was that the core Liberal vote – the lower-middle-class and upper-working-class man – did not suffer at all, right up to the outbreak of war. For men earning £500 to £1,000 a year, the tax take as a percentage of income was lower in 1913–14 than it had been in 1903–4 (Daunton 2001: 369–70). Between 1888 and 1914, the proportion of revenue obtained from direct taxation, overwhelmingly on the wealthiest, rose from 44 to 60 per cent (Emy 1973: 233–4).

However, Liberals did tax working men in another way, but they hypothecated it for a particular benefit and called it national insurance. Lloyd George announced in 1909 that a health insurance scheme would be introduced, and it was established in 1911. All insured workers between 16 and 70 earning less than the income tax threshold (£160 per year) were to be covered by a compulsory contribution scheme of 4d a week, which would provide a weekly benefit during illness. The aim was to provide a temporary cushion for the working man; dependent wives and children were not covered, and a sum to cover medical treatment was only added at a late stage. The contributions were not popular, and from a tax perspective were regressive: they pressed most heavily on the low paid, whereas many better-paid employees were already enrolled in friendly society schemes of this nature, which the state now subsidized (Searle 2004: 366–75; Daunton 2001: 366).

The scheme was advocated partly for its economic benefits. It would not disrupt the normal working of the market economy; indeed the aim was to improve "national efficiency" by reducing days off work and improving productivity, especially given the rising anxiety about a possible war with Germany, where social insurance was well established. The other benefit was on the debate about the Poor Law. The government regarded health and unemployment insurance (see page 40), along with old age pensions, as major steps towards lowering the poor relief burden. The government had no intention of overhauling the whole Poor Law, which would have absorbed a vast amount of political energy. It was able to dodge the issue because the Royal Commission on the subject set up in 1905 was divided, producing two clashing reports in 1909. The insurance schemes aimed to make the Poor Law a secondary political issue: a safety net for those in poverty who hardly mattered politically, as they lacked the vote.

Lloyd George intended the 1914 budget to be a further stage in the tackling of ratepayer grievances, but now as part of a bold land

Postcard published by the National Union of Conservative and Constitutional Associations, 1912. Teacher John Bull watches David Lloyd George, dressed as a ragged schoolboy, misspelling "Taxation for Revenue" as "Taxation for Revenge".

Source: SocialHistoryImages/Alamy Stock Photo.

campaign, which he launched in 1912–14 in the hope of finding the party's next great cause. As Ian Packer has shown, Liberals had already hoped in 1906 to use the land issue to secure their position in rural seats, but their flagship policy, an Act of 1907 to facilitate the purchase of smallholdings by the ambitious agricultural labourer, fell flat: only 2 per cent of labourers applied for them, and the party lost over half its English rural seats in 1910. Lloyd George's second attempt was based on the galvanizing effect of the land tax issue at the 1910 elections, when the Georgist song "The Land" was regularly sung at election meetings (as it was at all subsequent Liberal Party Assemblies). He now tried to link land reform to rural regeneration through offering better housing and the introduction of a minimum wage. Land taxation would unlock revenue that could reverse the drift of people to towns in search of work, which had increased overcrowding and urban unemployment (Packer 2001). The land valuation register inaugurated in 1909 was intended to pave the way for a 20 per cent tax on increases in value whenever land was sold. This would boost local authorities' coffers and allow them to invest in public health, education and housing. In the 1914 budget, substantial grants were promised to local authorities; Lloyd George promised these would deliver a rebate of 9d in the pound to the ratepayer. Logically these should have been funded by the new land taxes promised in 1909. This was impossible because the land value register was not ready. Lloyd George had to fall back on funding them by income tax increases on the wealthy, to which a group of low-tax Liberal MPs objected, forcing the abandonment of the bulk of the plan.

In the event, a more significant pointer for the future was the establishment of two funds – the Development Fund and Road Fund – in the 1909 budget. They were funded by central taxation rather than by loans because they were not intended to earn a return. They provided local authorities with funds for investment in land reclamation, afforestation, agricultural research, smallholdings and rural roads. As these grants could be timed to counteract the fluctuations of the trade cycle, the funds showed the beginnings of an interest in discretionary economic management (Sloman 2015: 25).

Liberal fiscal management was a major political success. Most income tax payers were no more heavily taxed than in 1905. Major extensions of welfare provision had been introduced and the burden on the ratepayer limited. The Liberals had secured free trade and the defence of the realm, and had maintained a cross-class coalition around the principle of low taxation. Government expenditure rose from £147 million in 1907 to £192 million in 1914, with the defence spending element rising by 30 per cent to £77 million. The Germans carried on their naval race, but the Admiralty maintained its advantage: Britain had 27 capital ships in the North Sea in July 1914 compared to Germany's 18.

However, the government could not maintain peace. Foreign Secretary Edward Grey hoped that all the powers would remain rational and conservative diplomatic players, but Germany wanted to pursue a revisionist agenda. Russia's weakness after its defeat by Japan in 1905 encouraged German ambitions. French concern about the rise of German power led to requests to Russia but also to Britain for more assistance. In several crises between 1905 and 1911, Germany tested the Anglo-French relationship, and Grey consistently gave France moral support and hints of military cooperation. He claimed that this did not mean hostility to Germany. Liberal backbenchers and newspaper editors were not convinced.

When the Balkan crisis of 1914 erupted, some in the British cabinet were tempted by talk of neutrality, but Grey – a Liberal Imperialist back in the 1890s – had no doubt that Britain would have to join in any European war. It could not risk a German victory leading to dominance in Europe and possible seizure of the French empire. Britain was under an obligation to defend the French Atlantic coast against Germany in return for France's naval support in the Mediterranean, which had become a French zone soon after the 1904 Anglo-French agreement. A good understanding with France remained a core element of British global power and the best security for a liberal world. Nor, given current imperial strains, was there any logic to making Russia an enemy. If Britain had remained neutral, and France and Russia had won the war, control of Egypt and India would have been badly jeopardized. This was all in addition to the treaty commitment of 1839 to defend the neutrality of Belgium, a key moment in the creation of the Anglo-French entente. Britain had too many global interests for other states not to cast covetous eyes on its possessions. Any war of the powers was bound to expose those possessions; that it was sparked off by rivalries in the distant Balkans was irrelevant. As throughout the last 80 years, some Liberals used Cobden's language of non-intervention, but it was not compatible with remaining a world power. The spirit of Palmerston still lived.

3

A pluralist politics? Religion, locality, Ireland and empire

Between 1828 and 1835, the old Tory political order in Britain was destroyed. This was not just because the 1832 Reform Act swept away nomination boroughs and made parliament much more accountable to public opinion. It was because legislation of 1828 and 1829 allowed Protestant Nonconformists and Roman Catholics to sit there.* Support for religious pluralism in the constitution, and particularly for "Catholic Emancipation", was the best signal of "liberalism" as the word was used in the 1820s.

Moreover, in 1835 the corporations that governed most important British towns were made accountable to local ratepayers through regular elections of councillors. The 1835 Municipal Corporations Act brought liberal politics to urban Britain. Unsurprisingly, it also ensured that the Liberal Party would dominate town politics. At local level, the Liberal Party rested overwhelmingly on the support of urban voters, many of whom were Protestant Nonconformists. As towns developed economically during the century, local Liberal associations became socially more diversified, without losing their political effectiveness.

Though these reforms strengthened the Liberal Party, they also forced it to behave in particular ways. A lot of power was devolved to local authorities. In principle, Liberals welcomed this. But how were the preferences of Protestant Nonconformity to be accommodated within a historically Anglican political system? And how could the defence of

* For simplicity, I have used the term "Nonconformist" to describe the members of the main historic Protestant sects outside the Established Church of England: Baptists, Congregationalists, Unitarians and Quakers (plus Wesleyan Methodists, although these were more prone to Toryism). Many people, especially before 1850, preferred to call these sects Dissent or Dissenters. Later, the term "Free Churchmen" was also popular.

local liberties and the interests of ratepayers be reconciled with central government anxieties about social order and good governance in the towns?

In Ireland, Liberals faced more acute problems. How were Irish Catholic interests to be reconciled with those of Protestants? And how were Irishmen to be persuaded to accept the Union with Britain? Finding the right principles on which to govern Ireland was the greatest challenge of Victorian Liberalism. It was a challenge not just because of the condition of Ireland and the legacies of history but also because Ireland was not a separate country. Liberal policies to Ireland needed to satisfy not just the Irish but also the British. If they did not, Liberal governments would lose power. Every electoral defeat of the Liberal Party after 1830 was due mainly to British people's dislike of its concessions to Ireland.

The desperate paradox of the 1800 Act of Union was that it made Ireland integral to Westminster politics while in other respects keeping it a colony. This was not the fault of the Liberal Party, but it had to deal with the legacy. The same is true of Liberal policy towards the British Empire. Some modern historians of empire ascribe the failings of the nineteenth-century British Empire to "Liberalism", as if all its actions and culture can be attributed to one dominant set of political assumptions. The reality was very different. Liberal governments inherited fundamental imperial problems, especially in the West Indies and India, where illiberal approaches to governance were entrenched. Very few Liberals thought that it was politically possible to remove these defects, given the state of those societies.

In some of the settler colonies, Liberal policy evolved towards upholding the principle of "self-government", and in 1886, Gladstone proposed this colonial model for Ireland. "Self-government" emerged relatively peacefully in Canada, but it was contested more in relation to New Zealand and South Africa, largely because of severe racial tensions there. (Australia fell somewhere between the two camps, and is omitted for space reasons.) Some London Liberals feared, rightly, that racist white settlers would manipulate self-governing institutions to deprive local indigenous peoples of property and rights. Evangelical Liberals made the case for British responsibility for the latter's protection. The principle of self-government tended to win out, because there was more consensus behind it at home, and it was cheaper. In the background of all these empire debates can be traced a general Liberal acquiescence in the assumption of the day: that some races had progressed to more advanced stages of civilisation than others. This added to the willingness to accept principles of imperial governance that Liberals would have been unwilling to contemplate for Britain itself.

Pluralism and the Nonconformist conscience

Until the 1820s, neither Protestant Nonconformists nor Roman Catholics were allowed to sit in parliament. The opposition Whig party attacked both exclusions, and the support of "Liberal" Tories helps to explain the passage of measures rectifying this in 1828 and 1829. In the 1830s, some Liberal MPs campaigned for Jews also to be allowed to sit in parliament. This issue became unavoidable with the election of the financier Lionel de Rothschild as MP for the City of London in 1847, since he could not take his seat without swearing a Christian oath of office. Revising the oath to allow Jewish MPs to swear it became a relatively non-partisan issue and was agreed in 1858.

There was more contention when the atheist and republican Charles Bradlaugh was elected Liberal MP for Northampton in 1880 and refused to swear the oath of allegiance. He asked for permission to make a non-religious affirmation instead, but Conservative MPs prevented any compromise. They exploited the Bradlaugh case for years, because they wanted to use it to raise doubts about Liberal support for both Church and Queen. The Conservative Party fought the 1885 election on a "Church in danger" campaign, provoked by the radical Joseph Chamberlain's call for Church disestablishment. This reflected continuing local constituency tensions between Anglican Tories and Liberal Nonconformists.

After 1832, Nonconformist lobby groups quickly urged reforms on the Liberal Party. To start with, the Protestant Dissenting Deputies took the lead, and in 1833 formed a United Committee with allied groups to ask the government to tackle six grievances. The Deputies were dominated by wealthy and philanthropical Unitarians, members of a minority elite in some of the country's most prosperous towns that rejected original sin and literal interpretations of the Bible. They believed that environment and hence education determined individuals' character.

William Smith, their leader from 1805 to 1832, inherited a great wholesale grocery business, bought 200 acres in Essex and three Rembrandts, sat in parliament for 45 years and perfected the image of a high-minded humanitarian reformer by urging the abolition of slavery and the removal of Nonconformist civil disabilities. One journalist commented that Unitarian leaders "were the only class of Dissenters known to the political coteries or clubs" (Machin 1977: 57). Their easy alliance with libertarian Whig aristocrats helped the governments of the 1830s to address some Nonconformist grievances. The Church's monopoly over the registration of births, marriages and deaths was removed. A charter to award degrees was granted to the non-religious University of London. Later, the right of non-Anglicans to take degrees at Oxford and Cambridge was secured by Liberal legislation, in 1854, 1856 and 1871. In 1833 and 1839, the government also introduced state grants and state inspection not only to Anglican elementary schools but also to others that taught the basics of Christianity on an "undenominational" basis.

However, one of the six grievances led to problems: the rates that the Church of England had historically levied on parishioners for church upkeep. It was not that Liberal ministers were unsympathetic to it: they brought in bills in 1834 and 1837 to abolish this compulsory charge, hoping to find the money needed from other sources, particularly the reforms to the Church's internal organization that an Ecclesiastical Commission was working on. But Church leaders would not cooperate with this strategy, and the bills were withdrawn. Meanwhile, radical Nonconformists began to mount campaigns of civil disobedience when charged the rate, and a couple of "martyrs" were jailed. The failure of Melbourne's government to resolve the issue created tensions with the more assertive Nonconformists at the 1841 election (Brent 1987). The Church rate issue petered out in the 1850s, after courts ruled that the rate could not be levied if a majority of the local vestry was opposed, and most Church authorities realized that making the rate a matter of local contention was counterproductive.

The episode showed that after the Reform Act the political leadership of Nonconformity was diversifying. The highly educated liberal Unitarian minority was losing dominance, as more spokesmen emerged for evangelical, middle-class Baptist and Congregationalist communities from provincial towns. Many of these were simultaneously involved in secular radical agitations on the Corn Laws and the franchise question. The Church rate issue prompted Edward Miall to create the *Nonconformist* newspaper in 1841 and the Anti-State Church Association in 1844, which was modelled on the Anti-Corn Law League. The Association was renamed the Liberation Society in 1853: it called for the disestablishment and disendowment of state Churches, and a rejection of all payments by taxpayers and ratepayers to the state for religious purposes.

This new principle went under various names: "religious equality", "voluntaryism" or "free trade in religion" (Larsen 1999). It was potentially a major problem for Liberal political leaders. The latter were almost all Anglicans who valued the Established Church as a vehicle for promoting morality in all social classes and for underpinning the authority and Christian responsibility of the political elite. Liberal Anglican historians such as Thomas Arnold and Connop Thirlwall pointed to the decay and degradation that had overwhelmed past empires, and argued that only the spread of Christian morality in a nation could defend against it. Palmerston and Russell were broad churchmen who hoped that a modern Church, not wedded to dogmas or rituals, could be a truly national and representative institution to fit the national, representative liberal state. Anglican Liberals also tended to think that the teaching of undenominational Christianity in ratepayer-funded schools was the best solution to the fraught question of the relationship between the state and religious education. In any case, as politicians they were aware that many Anglican voters regarded disestablishment with horror, as a step towards social anarchy.

Radical Nonconformists, however, rejected the idea of state Churches as socially divisive, potentially tyrannical, complacent and unchristian. They saw individual conscience as the best antidote to sin and materialism; they thought that a priesthood denied that freedom and undercut Christ's authority, but that state claims of authority over the Church did so as well. They felt that the alliance with the state corrupted the Church's purity and spiritual zeal, while the search for a national appeal led it to fudge doctrinal truth. Rather than keeping the nation faithful to the gospel of Christ, it prevented it from becoming a great community conscientiously searching for religious virtue. England without its Established Church would be more religious, not less. Many Nonconformists believed that their ancestors, led by Oliver

Cromwell, had secured the religious purity of Britain in the civil wars of the seventeenth century (Parry 2006: 113–17).

In practice, Nonconformists' zeal for voluntaryism depended on how dissatisfied they were with politics in general. In the 1840s economic depressions, radical suspicion of the oppressiveness and sectionalism of the state was at its height. In 1847, Russell's government ignored intense voluntaryist opposition and extended state grants for elementary school teacher training and books; Catholic schools were also included. Meanwhile the government's dependence on Anglican Peelites for its majority prevented it from settling the Church rate issue.

Another highpoint of Nonconformists' enthusiasm was around 1867. They convinced themselves that the Second Reform Act would create a disinterested political order in which all religious vested interests could be swept away. They regarded Gladstone's campaign for disestablishment and disendowment of the Irish Church in 1868 as a noble first step. But they were also alarmed at the religious compromises embedded in the 1870 Education Act, and at Irish Roman Catholics' demands for university funding. They responded with a campaign for the complete separation of religious teaching and state funding, and for the disestablishment of the Church of England. In 1871–3, this nearly paralysed the Liberal Party and prompted a great reaction of Anglican voters in favour of the Conservatives (Parry 2006: 301–11).

This, however, was the last powerful flourish of Nonconformist anti-statism. Nonconformists believed, like most Liberals, that the diffusion of power had made the post-1867 state more trustworthy than the pre-1848 one. Once the system of elected school boards was established, most of these men came to accept whatever pragmatic policy for Bible teaching the boards agreed, and by the 1880s it was mostly Catholics and Anglicans who insisted that individual parental conscience should override a democratic mandate on children's religious education (Handcock 1977: 510–16). Moreover, most Nonconformists were never entirely comfortable with the old radical strategy of blaming aristocratic politicians for national failures, thinking instead that each member of a Christian community had a responsibility to improve its virtue.

Nonconformists certainly did not become complacent about politics. Indeed after 1867, many of them feared that democracy might turn secular unless properly directed. Leading it into Christian paths would allow it to fulfil its sacred mission. Voters should be taught by example the importance of taking responsibility for the ethical state of the nation. They adopted several issues that seemed particularly suited to teach this lesson. One was the attempt to limit the damage done to individuals, families and society by excessive drinking. From 1853, a United Kingdom Alliance took up the temperance issue, aiming to "infuse a new morality into state-action". For decades, it campaigned for legislation to allow a majority of ratepayers in any district to ban the drink trade from their locality (Harrison 1970: 375). Another moral cause was the successful campaign against the Contagious Diseases Acts, which had condoned a system of prostitution in garrison towns and forced women to endure demeaning inspections and incarceration; it seemed illiberal, amoral, sexist and un-English (Roberts 2004: 213–18, 250–56). Nonconformists were heavily involved in the agitation that arose in 1876 in protest at Ottoman Muslim atrocities against Bulgarian Christians, particularly once the press exposed large-scale cruelty and some child rape (Bebbington 1982: 115). They asserted that conscience rather than official and elite convenience should determine foreign policy, and that voters should expect leaders to show an appropriately Christian spirit in handling it, which seemed entirely lacking in the Jewish Prime Minister Disraeli. Many were also outraged by the continuation of the slave trade in all parts of Africa, and felt that Britain had an obligation to intervene to stop it.

Lloyd George's appeal to Nonconformists was founded on rhetorical powers that were shaped by his childhood in north Wales and his Baptist preacher uncle. The first stage in the Liberal revival that culminated in the landslide victory of 1906 was the nostalgia-laden campaign against the Conservatives' 1902 Education Act, which abolished elected school boards and placed all schools under local education authorities, irrespective of their religious status. This destroyed the 1870 compromise, under which schools run by the Church of England or by Roman Catholics rather than by local boards were not to be funded by local ratepayers. Encouraged by Lloyd George, nearly all the Welsh local education authorities refused to enforce the Act, a campaign that led into a movement for Welsh Church disestablishment. In England, about 10,000 Nonconformists (out of two million) mounted a campaign of passive resistance, refusing to pay for "Rome on the rates". When their goods were seized in lieu, many chose to surrender their electroplated teapots, which friends would buy back at auction (Munson 1991:

263–76). At the 1906 election, 157 Nonconformists were returned as Liberal MPs.

Community and local politics

Because the Church of England was weak in most towns, the 1835 Municipal Corporations Act gave Nonconformists access to a lot of local power. In Leeds, they provided all the mayors for the next ten years; in Leicester, they occupied two-thirds of council seats (Machin 1977: 55). More broadly, Liberals dominated urban local government for most of the century, but they disagreed among themselves on many things. Urban politics involved a constant battle between two main types of Liberal: improvers and cost-cutters. Improvers tended to be members of local elites with a religious or social conscience or a professional expertise in law or medical science. Their hopes of doing more to regulate sanitary conditions, education and policing were buttressed by helpful guidance issued by expert civil servants in central government. Cost-cutters were businessmen and ratepayers who distrusted those initiatives as too expensive and too dictatorial.

The 1835 Act opened the government of 178 towns that had corporate borough status, by requiring them all to be run primarily by councillors regularly elected by ratepayers. Lots of corporations had become self-perpetuating closed bodies, which the reformers of 1835 regarded as vested interests. This was, firstly, because many corporations regarded their main job as to manipulate the election of local MPs, until most of these "rotten boroughs" were abolished in 1832. Corporations also had the power to select local magistrates, with the result that populations did not always trust them to administer justice, contributing to the risk of disorder. They might lack gravitas: one East Retford magistrate, it was claimed, chatted with culprits brought to court and fought with a prisoner. In Bristol, they were mostly non-resident, thus in Liberal eyes explaining the breakdown of order there in 1831. Finally, local economies often suffered from corporate carelessness: a Royal Commission of 1833 uncovered stories of absurdly high duties imposed on particular goods, or favoured families gaining benefit from the use of the corporation's own charitable trusts. Collectively, corporations were £1.86 million in debt, which meant that ratepayers who could not vote them out had to cover their high interest charges (Parry 1993: 116–19).

As with the Reform Act itself, the assumption behind the 1835 Act was that local taxpayers would tend to choose respectable men who cared about the town and would administer its affairs judiciously yet economically. This would create what Prime Minister Melbourne called a "community of feeling" between townspeople and their councillors (Hansard 14 August 1835: 495). Councillors would choose local magistrates. Each corporation must also appoint a watch committee to manage a paid police force, and the committee was to report quarterly to the Home Office. So at a stroke almost every major town was required to have an efficient police force. At this point, worry about urban disorder drove much of the concern for better government. The Act also stopped corporations from exempting individuals from dues or awarding favoured people trading rights, and brought in central government regulation of purchases or leases of corporate property. This was another attack on "old corruption".

Initially, the powers of urban local government were strictly limited. The trigger for expansion was panic about the "condition of England" in the 1840s and specifically the cholera outbreak of 1848–9, which exposed the lack of a reliable water supply and the inadequacy of sewage and burial practices in severely overcrowded towns. The Russell government's Public Health Act of 1848 encouraged towns to set up elected local boards of health, which could raise rates to construct and manage sewers, drains and water supply. They were to be supervised by the General Board in London, which had the power to enforce a local board on reluctant ratepayers in towns where death rates were high. Many towns already had improvement commissions, bodies of concerned citizens who had got parliament to allow them to raise a local rate for communal water supply and gas lighting. Where these existed, they often now reconstituted themselves as local boards.

By 1858, there were 219 local boards of health. But this was often a costly initiative and therefore controversial for ratepayers. When Leicester adopted the Public Health Act in 1848, the borough rate tripled in a year. An Act of 1846 allowed local boroughs and parishes to levy a rate to build public baths and washhouses, and Acts of 1850 and 1855 made the same possible for public libraries, but by 1865 only 33 and 24 authorities had done this. Partly because of the cost, only

31 towns applied to become incorporated self-governing boroughs between 1835 and 1865, including Birmingham and Manchester (Parry 1993: 206).

The decisive decades for the creation of a more active culture of urban local government were the two after the 1867 Reform Act, when local elites and central government worked together to improve the social order and social health of towns. In 1871, Gladstone's government set up the Local Government Board (LGB), amalgamating the departments previously responsible for the Poor Law and public health. In 1872, the LGB created a comprehensive network of local sanitary authorities, each with specific obligations and a medical officer. In towns, the corporations or boards of health became these authorities, and outside them the boards of guardians did. The LGB audited and thus validated the spending of local authorities; this gave them the security for a massive programme of borrowing against the rates for infrastructural improvement. Loans to local authorities rose from £7.4 million in 1858–71 to £31.5 million in 1871–84. Aided by the widespread use of parliamentary provisional order legislation, local authorities gained powers to put gas, water and electricity under municipal control. This also made them profits, which could be sunk into further investments, such as libraries, parks and the great town halls and art galleries that appeared as symbols of civic pride in Manchester, Birmingham, Leeds, Liverpool and Bradford. Between 1870 and 1882, local government expenditure rose from £27.3 million to £55.5 million (Parry 1993: 238–9).

A parallel development across England in these years was the attempt by government to reform privately-endowed corporate bodies in the public interest. These included 782 endowed schools, which were scrutinized by a Royal Commission of 1864–7, the Taunton Commission. Nearly all schools that educated teenage children had been created as private charities, with restricted endowments of various kinds. So the education they provided was limited to particular subjects, while access to it was confined to particular professions or localities. After the Commission reported, Gladstone's government set up an Endowed Schools Commission in 1869, with the aim of modernizing and liberalizing these endowed bodies for public benefit. The same philosophy shaped the embryonic higher education sector. In 1870, an Act re-established Owens' College, which aspired to provide a higher education in Manchester, "under the management of a public body rather than of trustees of private nomination". Its new constitution, drafted by James Bryce, one of the Taunton Commissioners, specified a strong local lay element in its governing body. This model of local lay involvement was replicated when it was reincarnated as the University of Manchester in 1880, and then replicated further in most civic universities established in the following few decades (Jones 2024).

The ethos of civic pride that developed in most substantial British towns was due partly to competition between them and partly to the spirit of assertive paternalism that many wealthy local businessmen embodied. Quite a few towns came to be associated with successful businesses that became household names: Colman's mustard in Norwich, Palmer's biscuits in Reading, Beecham's pills in St Helens, Boot's the chemist in Nottingham, Rank's flour in Hull, Peter Taylor the Leicester silk magnate. Most men of this stamp provided their town with major philanthropic donations even if they did not go into politics (Munson 1991).

Many local political leaders came from networks of wealthy Unitarian families. Their belief in the value of a scientific and moral education predisposed them to devote time to public service, sanitary improvement and improved facilities for popular education and rational recreation. Such men (and women) sought by example to educate more selfish businessmen and cheapskate ratepayers into a more elevated idea of local politics. The Liverpool Unitarian merchant and MP William Rathbone insisted that wealth was not a gift to be enjoyed by selfish individuals but a sacred trust to be employed for the welfare of the community (Munson 1991: 31). In Birmingham, the municipalization programme of the 1870s was the first great political campaign of the Unitarian businessman Joseph Chamberlain. Chamberlain and his colleagues built on the charismatic preaching of the city's heterodox pastor George Dawson, who told his congregations that the town was "a solemn organism through which should flow, and in which should be shaped all the highest, loftiest and truest ends of man's moral nature" (Hennock 1973: 75, 161–2).

Although he had lost his religious faith, T. H. Green, a university teacher in Oxford and a member of the Oxford town council in the 1870s, is best seen as a figure with similar aspirations. He was determined to teach his students the benefits of community work, through political activity or through the sort of social service that his pupil Arnold Toynbee undertook among the poor in Whitechapel (which was commemorated in the establishment of Toynbee Hall after his death). His vision of political participation targeted vested interests that prevented human beings from being able to realize their best selves. The battle could be fought through school boards or local government: Green was the first Oxford college Fellow to sit on the town council, aiming to break down social barriers. It could also be fought through the volunteer temperance associations that combatted the brewers, or through the university extension movement (Richter 1964: 345–6). Ultimately, Green hoped, so many individuals would be socialized into law-abiding civic activity that there would be no need for a coercive state. Green, like Toynbee, died very young, but his communitarianism influenced many of his students.

In 1886, the leading Liberal politician Lord Hartington declared that the "extension of popular self-government all over the country" was a firm Liberal principle (Parry 1993: 241). This indicated a desire to use the 1884 Reform Act as a lever to liberalize the counties as well as the boroughs. That desire was frustrated by the split in the party over Irish Home Rule, with the result that county government reform was left to the Conservative Party, which introduced a modest scheme of county councils (1888). Nonetheless, the slow organic increase of urban powers through the nineteenth century was an important element of Liberal government practice. The state prompted this process but hardly ever dictated it. Private corporate entities were "municipalized" into possessing a public ethos. Most of these entitles were elected: councillors, boards of health and, after 1870, school boards. Their popular accountability helped to defuse many political issues that would otherwise have been politically difficult for the party. Liberal intellectuals such as Green, or later L. T. Hobhouse, described the aim of Liberalism as the socialization of individuals into civil society without the intervention of a heavy-handed state that would suppress the energy and self-control that was the essence of their individuality (Hobhouse 1911: 123, 130, 146, 232–3). These writings sound more utopian and radical than they were. They were elegant ways of describing social arrangements that were increasingly visible in many towns by the end of the century.

Catholicism and Ireland

In Britain, Liberals assumed that local elites should be entrusted with power. In Ireland, they lacked confidence in the reliability, good sense or patriotism of nearly all those who demanded a share of it. Liberals were convinced that the Tory Protestant landed elite could never keep the Catholic Irish contented, but they did not think that Catholic bishops, Nationalist demagogues or Fenian agitators could be trusted with government at all. As a result, Liberals remained reluctant to address the fundamental issue: whether it was safe to dismantle the colonial governance institutions that previous regimes had imposed on Ireland. They did, however, try to tackle what they saw as the great vested interest of Protestant landed power.

In 1800, Pitt and Castlereagh engineered an Act of Union to tie Ireland more firmly to Britain during the French wars. Encouraged by leading Irish Protestants, George III insisted, against Pitt's advice, that his coronation oath forbade him to allow Catholics to be members of the new United Kingdom Parliament. Meanwhile the government retained a Lord Lieutenant of Ireland, with an official residence in Phoenix Park: a representative of Crown power, which Wales and Scotland did not need. The Lord Lieutenant presided over an administration based in Dublin Castle. From 1814, that administration appointed an armed police force of over 5,000 men, which became a county constabulary in 1822. There was no similar force in Britain (and the one introduced in English municipal boroughs in 1835 was unarmed and subject to the control of elected authorities). It was housed in strategically placed barracks in areas of most potential unrest. Moreover, it supplemented the presence of 20,000 British troops, which many British politicians would have liked to remove but could not do without.

After Catholic Emancipation was conceded in 1829, a numerous Irish Catholic parliamentary grouping led by Daniel O'Connell quickly emerged. Catholics also mounted a largely non-violent protest at the requirement to pay tithes to the minority Established Anglican Church in Ireland. The Established Church provided jobs for 22 bishops and numerous other dignitaries but served a population of only 850,000. It was easy to present it as an example of "old corruption" and greed. In 1833, Grey's government removed 12 of the bishoprics but disagreed on whether parliament could and should "appropriate" some of its revenues for broader Irish purposes. The initial reform was accompanied by a stringent Coercion Act allowing the Lord Lieutenant to suppress civil liberties in districts that he deemed "disturbed". In 1834–5, ministers split badly on whether this was an acceptable basis on which to govern Ireland.

This crisis created a recognizable parliamentary Liberal Party. The government formed in 1835 by Lord Melbourne was defined by new principles that disquieted former Prime Minister Grey and former Irish Secretary Lord Stanley. These were that Ireland must be governed by an understanding with O'Connell; that all future Coercion Acts must be accompanied by a meaningful reform programme to tackle the excessive powers of the Protestant Tory landed elite; and that a popularly elected parliament had the right and duty to reallocate Church endowments, in the public interest. Lord John Russell, the leader of the new government in the House of Commons, called the Protestant landlords a "miserable monopolising minority" (Hansard 7 February 1837: 221). The new Liberal perspective was based on the reality of Irish politics, but it also indicated the party's great dilemma. The support of O'Connell's MPs shored up its majority in parliament and at the same time endangered it. British Protestant hostility to a pro-Catholic Liberal Party drove the reaction in favour of Conservatism, which weakened the Liberals' position at the 1835 election, almost removed their majority in 1837 and destroyed it in 1841.

Over the 80 years after 1835, the Liberal Party did not always have the enthusiasm for coherent solutions to the Irish policy dilemma, but there were three main attempts at finding one. The first was the gambit of Russell and his allies, between 1835 and 1852; the second was Gladstone's between 1866 and 1874; and the third was the Home Rule strategy that was pursued intermittently from 1885 onwards.

Russell's aim was to boost Irish popular confidence in the British state and the Union, through regular dialogue and informal understandings with the leaders of Catholic political and religious opinion. There would be large numbers of Catholic appointments to political and judicial office and the police force. The state would seek to check the landlords' abuses of power and to force them to accept their responsibilities to their tenants. It would also accept the Catholic Church's dominant standing among the Irish people and would offer the Irish priesthood more financial security. Like many Whigs, Russell supported the principle of "concurrent endowment" by the state of all Irish religions: the granting of financial support to Catholics along with Presbyterians and Episcopalians. The hope was to enhance the status, social independence and loyalty of the Catholic clergy, to demonstrate the state's commitment to religious pluralism, to signal support for the social and moral work of all denominations and to solve Catholics' grievances without removing the Anglican Church Establishment (Parry 2001–2).

The government of 1835–41 enhanced Catholic representation in parliament, local government, the administration, the police and the magistracy. It appointed six Catholics to government office, reformed the Irish police force (bringing in many Catholics) and removed large numbers of Protestant magistrates. Municipal reform, in 1840, secured Catholic leadership in Dublin (where O'Connell was elected Lord Mayor in 1841), although the House of Lords greatly limited the scope of the legislation. The introduction of a Poor Law in Ireland in 1838 made the landlords responsible for poor relief; it was hoped that they would invest in agriculture to minimize their relief burdens. O'Connell wrote that the government was "conquering the 'anti-Saxon' Spirit of Ireland" (Scherer 1999: 97). But the Conservative opposition in the Lords, aware of British anti-Catholic sentiment, was able to kill the government's more ambitious plans: neither "appropriation", nor Russell's plan of 1838 to endow the Catholic priests, got anywhere.

When the Liberals returned to government in 1846, with Russell as prime minister, Ireland was in deep crisis, yet the government had even less room for manoeuvre. Russell lacked a firm majority in the Commons, while Irish MPs had no leader who could organize a popular campaign after O'Connell died in 1847. Moreover, British opinion had become more performatively anti-Catholic. Not just evangelical Anglicans but also many Protestant Nonconformists vehemently opposed state financial support for the Catholic seminary at Maynooth, which ensured that Russell's attempt at a scheme of "concurrent endowment" in 1847–8 was a non-starter.

Meanwhile the Irish bishops, led by Archbishop Paul Cullen, assumed the role of spokesmen for Irish Catholicism. Cullen was particularly opposed to the idea – advocated by Peel as well as Russell – that the Church, or the pope, should enter into understandings with the British state. Cullen opposed the mixed higher education colleges, the Queen's Colleges, which the Peel government had set up in 1845, and which Russell wanted to extend into an interdenominational Irish university. He summoned a Synod at Thurles in 1850 to condemn the Colleges as injurious to the faith and morals of Catholics, seeing them, rightly, as a British attempt to emancipate middle-class Catholics from clerical influence. Russell was a proud man, and the defeat of his various strategies explains his disastrous attack on the Catholic bishops in his Durham Letter of November 1850 and Ecclesiastical Titles Act of 1851. The cause was the pope's declaration that he had established a hierarchy of 12 Catholic bishops in England. Russell claimed that the Roman Church was trying to put itself above the rule of state law. His declaration ruined his reputation as a friend to Ireland, and marked the virtual death knell of his strategy (Kerr 1994).

His government had also struggled badly to respond to the Irish famine which resulted from the failure of the potato crop in 1845 and succeeding years. British public opinion was intensely hostile to major relief packages for Ireland, and a weak government, itself divided on how generous to be, lacked the power to overcome it. The hostility derived partly from ideological objections, fringed with racism, to generous grants to an Irish people who in the words of *The Times* suffered from "innate indolence". The Treasury's head civil servant, Charles Trevelyan, held these views rigidly (Gray 1999). Many Liberals also believed that grants would go into the pockets of unscrupulous landlords, so government tried to force the landlords to take more responsibility for the relief of their tenants. Moreover, the depression of 1847–8 intensified British radicals' demands for lower government expenditure and for tax cuts, which the government lacked the majority to resist. Indeed the banking crisis of 1847 was widely blamed on "extravagant" expenditure on the Irish (Read 2022). Russell lamented that the reason for the Irish famine policy failure "lies deep in the breast of the British people" (Kerr 1994: 198).

By the 1860s, the increasing political influence of evangelical voluntaryist Nonconformists forced the Liberal Party to turn away from Russell's policy of binding Catholics into alliance with the state. In 1867–9, the new Liberal leader Gladstone set out and then enacted a policy founded on the idea of Church disestablishment and disendowment (and abolition of the Maynooth grant). At the 1868 election, Gladstone revisited the critique of the Irish Church that had created the party in 1835, but now with an explicit commitment to disestablishment and state disinterestedness in Irish religious matters. Liberals accused the Conservatives of wanting to support multiple established Churches and a state-funded Catholic university. Gladstone's rejection of concurrent endowment – the pacification of interest groups by state reallocation of Church property – together with his rigid views on spending cuts also led him to reduce Russell's emphasis on patronage as a tool in Irish politics. When the Irish Home Rule movement began in 1870, one initial theme was that Gladstone's penny-pinching government was neglecting local Irish job needs (Parry 2006: 262–6).

Gladstone's policy of "justice to Ireland" also included a Land Act of 1870 that steered Irish landlords to atone for past confiscations of tenant property. It sought to impose a social contract between landlord and tenant, based on "Irish ideas": on local customary traditions known as "Ulster custom" that in practice secured tenure, and the right to sell the land on, as long as a fair rent was paid. These traditions were given legal recognition wherever they could be proved to exist. In other places, courts were established to negotiate a working relationship between landlord and tenant.

In British eyes, however, the Catholic problem grew rather than diminished after disestablishment. At the Vatican Council in 1870, the pope asserted his "infallibility" in determining what doctrines Catholics should accept. British Nonconformists, meanwhile, were protesting at clauses in the government's 1870 Education Act that they feared Catholic schools would exploit to strengthen their position. When Irish bishops demanded a Catholic university, anxiety in Britain mounted. Gladstone's compromise solution for Irish universities fell between stools, offending the bishops but also many British liberals because of restrictions on the syllabus to reflect Catholic theological sensitivities. When his Irish University Bill was defeated in 1873, his government was fatally damaged. Sympathy between British Liberals and Irish Catholics had broken down. Gladstone ended in the same place as Russell: after his defeat at the 1874 election, he attacked the papacy for interfering with Catholic laymen's hearts and minds (Parry 2006: 318–20).

A major objective of Russell's and Gladstone's differing approaches to Irish Catholicism was to establish conditions in which a propertied pro-Union Irish Catholic lay political class could emerge and flourish. Many local landowners – the O'Conor Don in Roscommon, the O'Donoghue in Tipperary, William Monsell in Limerick – hoped to play this role, but after 1874 they were marginalized (Enright 2022). Liberal failure in Ireland was signalled by the emergence of a strong Home Rule movement instead.

From the late 1870s, one wing of this, under Charles Stewart Parnell, became associated with aggressive political initiatives, both in parliament – obstructing parliamentary debates by marathon speeches – and outside it, where his Land League developed the tactic of boycotting landlords who refused to reduce rents and tried to evict tenants. When Gladstone returned to government in 1880 and brought in a further instalment of land reform, Parnell attacked it as inadequate. The government accompanied its 1881 Land Act by a Coercion Act, under which Parnell was imprisoned for sabotage, but he was then controversially released from jail in 1882. The government's Irish Secretary Forster resigned at tactics that seemed to make Parnell the ringmaster of political stability. Much of the British press responded to Irish unrest by painting the people as undisciplined, irresponsible and lawless, often using racial stereotypes. In October 1880, Chamberlain noted British workmen's annoyance at Parnell: they "do not like to see the law set at defiance". John Morley felt – just like Russell in 1848 – that the difficulties in Irish policy were "due to the British public" (Parry 2006: 380).

The enlarged Irish electorate voted overwhelmingly for nationalist candidates at the 1885 election that followed the Third Reform Act, and Parnell now held the balance of power at Westminster. Ironically, this was because Ireland had almost twice as many parliamentary seats as its population ratio would indicate, an imbalance that was justified by the lack of representative local government. In response, Gladstone proposed Home Rule: the re-establishment of the Irish Parliament that the Act of Union had abolished. This move, which he had not mentioned before the election, stunned the whole political class. It was a deliberate attempt to make himself the arbiter of politics and the indispensable leader of the party. Liberal MPs were forced either to support it or oppose it. The Conservatives alleged that this was a simple and immoral bid for the votes of lawless Irish Nationalists in order to become prime minister.

Gladstone did not think he was doing the Nationalists' bidding. He considered most Nationalist MPs unscrupulous and ungentlemanly, like "vermin about a man's person" (Parry 2006: 374). One aim of his Home

Rule scheme was to undermine their appeal and restore the leadership of a civic-minded propertied Irish elite, which he convinced himself had been unfairly robbed of power by the Act of Union. Gladstone argued that Ireland was a British outgrowth, a settler colony like Canada and the Australian states, which deserved the same self-government that those places had been awarded in the 1840s and 1850s, when they rightly resisted feeble and high-taxing executive government from London. Colonies should be self-governing municipal corporations. Irish MPs had been able to pressure the Treasury into giving local interest groups special benefits and doles, but self-government would educate them and Irish voters into electoral and fiscal responsibility (Loughlin 1986).

The Irish question became the latest of the single-issue causes that justified Gladstone's continuance in politics. The fact that Home Rule was unlikely to be won any time soon was among its attractions for him; it offered a satisfyingly immersive and prolonged struggle. But 94 Liberal MPs voted against his Home Rule Bill and defeated it. They hoped he would resign as party leader; instead he tied the party to support his policy at the 1886 election, and Liberal dissidents – now called Liberal Unionists – were left looking for a new political home.

Liberal opposition to Home Rule was driven by a mixture of political and principled arguments. At root, opponents thought it was an enormous gift to the Conservative Party. It was easy to present Home Rule as a concession to a movement based on lawlessness and outrage. Some Unionists claimed that an Irish parliament would be dominated by populist sentiments against property-owners, whereas the duty of Westminster was to maintain throughout the length and breadth of the empire the undisputed supremacy of the law. The scheme reserved defence, foreign affairs and trade powers to Westminster; would Nationalists accept that, or lobby for complete separation? Unionists feared that Home Rule would damage imperial strength at a time of international competition.

The Liberal Unionist secession was led by Lord Hartington and Joseph Chamberlain. They and many of their parliamentary followers ended in alliance with the Conservative Party; both men were leading members of Lord Salisbury's Conservative and Unionist cabinet from 1895. But neither intended in 1886 to leave the party to which he had devoted his career. They hoped that Gladstone, who was 76, would be forced out instead, and that the party would prefer to prioritize

An 1889 cartoon by John Tenniel depicting William Gladstone trying to coax all the main players in the Irish Question into the centre of his shamrock puzzle

Source: World History Archive / Alamy Stock Photo.

other issues. Chamberlain had developed a modernizing programme of social and institutional reform, which he was convinced, rightly, that Gladstone hated. Neither Hartington nor Chamberlain believed that the status quo in Ireland could endure. They understood that any future Liberal government would have to respond to Irish pressure with major reforms. These were likely to include significant democratization of Irish local government and a comprehensive land purchase package to buy out underinvesting landlords. Capital investment schemes were mooted, for example in Irish railways and tramways (Parry 2006: 381–5).

As it was, Gladstone's commitment to his socially conservative brand of Home Rule put his party on the back foot electorally. It helped to ensure Conservative dominance of British politics for 20 years. Gladstone returned to government in 1892, only courtesy of Irish Nationalist support, and introduced a Home Rule Bill in 1893, which the Unionist majority in the Lords defeated overwhelmingly on the grounds that there was no nationwide popular mandate for it. Parnell's career had been destroyed in 1890 when he was named as co-respondent in a divorce case. British Nonconformists who had recently been campaigning against prostitution and vice refused to accept that a man "convicted of immorality" should lead a parliamentary party (Bebbington 1982: 100–1). Nationalists won power at local level in much of Ireland, while the Conservatives' 1903 Land Purchase Act removed many of the old landlords and reduced landlord–tenant tensions. Moreover, when the Liberals returned to power in 1905–6, it was with such a large electoral majority that they did not need to prioritize Ireland.

So the power balance after 1906 between the Liberal government and the Irish Nationalist parliamentary leader John Redmond was completely different to that between Gladstone and Parnell in 1885. Redmond accepted the leadership's planned step-by-step approach and agreed not to demand Home Rule in the 1906 parliament. The Liberals proposed instead a programme of local government reform, university reform and financial aid for overcrowded districts.

The problem with this strategy was that it opened Redmond to criticism from his opponents within Ireland. The attack on denominational education in the Liberals' 1906 Education Bill (for England) offended Catholics, while the extension of local government in the Irish Councils Bill allowed Redmond's rivals in Ireland to suggest that his strategy was undermining the nationalist cause. As a result, Redmond was forced to terminate his cooperation with the government and to revert to demanding Home Rule, so as to hold the political centre in Ireland: to see off the threat to his position from Sinn Fein and a faction led by William O'Brien. Events then worked in Redmond's favour, because his MPs secured the balance of power at Westminster after the 1910 elections. Asquith could no longer dodge the Home Rule issue (O'Day 1979).

Meanwhile the passage of the 1911 Parliament Act meant that the Lords could only delay a Home Rule Bill for two parliamentary sessions. This meant that Home Rule became an early vehicle for concern about the newly unfettered power of executive government. This concern made advance discussion of the terms of any bill extremely fraught, as its potential consequences and implications were considered in much more detail than they had been when it seemed unlikely to pass. Opponents raised two concerns in particular: for Protestant Ulster, which clearly did not wish to be subjugated to a Dublin Parliament; and about the consequences of the bill for Britain's imperial status. Supporters argued that Home Rule would not only be an act of democratic fairness to Ireland but would also allow a more efficient constitutional balance, allowing local measures to be discussed locally and imperial ones centrally.

Even more than in the past, the debates focused on British and imperial needs more than Irish ones. The idea of some sort of federal system for the UK – "Home Rule all round" – was discussed in cross-party talks in 1910, in the hope that it might help the management of parliamentary business, remove the sense that the Irish were getting special treatment and limit the risk of further Irish agitation for complete independence. The Irish Nationalists naturally opposed the idea but only managed to defeat the final version of it – in which local bills affecting the interests of the various United Kingdom regions would be debated by grand committees of regional MPs – in March 1912. Meanwhile the government was very slow to appreciate the grievances of Ulster. Lloyd George and Churchill asked for special terms for Ulster in 1912, but Asquith did not see the need for them (Jalland 1979). The government gave no indication of a concession until March 1914, by which time Edward Carson and the Unionists had fomented a lot of opposition in the province. Asquith proposed the exclusion of six Ulster counties for a fixed number of years, to be followed by a plebiscite (Jackson 2003: 128–9). Heightened tensions in Ulster prevented progress on that issue, but Asquith seems to have been confident that the Unionists would not support a rebellion (Jackson 2003: 140–1). In the summer of 1914, the Government of Ireland Act finally passed into law, and discussions were promised about the "temporary" exemption of Ulster. The outbreak of war meant instead that the whole Act was suspended. The war and the 1916 Easter Rising then changed the political parameters, gave Sinn Fein the leadership of Irish opinion and inaugurated a military struggle for independence. This resulted in the creation of a separate Irish Free State (within the British Empire) excluding the six counties of Northern Ireland, which were separately given substantial self-government from 1921.

How should Liberal strategies for Ireland be assessed? Most Liberals did not want to acknowledge the case for Irish nationalism or the irremediable separateness of Ireland. Nor was Irish nationalism a permanent political problem for them; only O'Connell, Parnell and Redmond gave it enough coherence to have real leverage at Westminster, and they only periodically. Liberals aimed to respond to generalized Irish discontent in ways that would work politically for Britain and Ireland at the same time. They were looking for a viable representative politics that would keep together a British–Irish coalition under Liberal leadership and on Liberal principles. The various solutions – appropriation, concurrent endowment, disestablishment, cautious land reform, a strikingly conservative Home Rule scheme – were shaped and limited by British at least as much as Irish pressures. In fact, none was very successful electorally, across the United Kingdom as a whole, because of Tory opposition. They should be judged as a form of political art, an attempt to find universalist liberal principles that could be imposed on Ireland, in the hope of salving British consciences and of reducing the offensiveness of the system that Liberals inherited in 1830 and never felt able to abolish.

Empire

Like the Act of Union, the British Empire predated the era of Liberal politics and was founded on different principles. The empire was a phenomenon created by trade and enterprise but also by conquest. Its military-political institutions were well entrenched before 1830. Liberal attempts after that date to reform it operated under severe constraints.

One colony particularly resistant to liberal politics, for example, was Jamaica, which had had an Assembly dominated by white planters since

1662. Liberal governments made two attempts to rein in the planter element. The first was the abolition of slavery, which an immensely strong abolitionist lobby in Britain demanded after the 1832 Reform Act had removed the planters' remaining influence in the Westminster parliament. In 1833, a few government members, led by Grey's son and heir Lord Howick, pressed for immediate abolition, in order to shock the planters into accepting a free market wage economy if they wanted continuing British protection. The cabinet disagreed and thought that stability required a compromise intermediate apprenticeship phase, which lasted until 1840. When Liberals returned to power in 1846, Howick, the new Lord Grey, imposed a variant of this shock tactic, a scheme of equalization of sugar duties. This aimed to remove the high tariffs against foreign sugar that had protected the Jamaican planters from competition. Pragmatic considerations meant that this equalization was also delayed, until 1854. The planters continued to control the economy and to oppress the labourers, through indenture schemes, heavy indirect taxes on former slaves, control of the justice system and electoral gerrymandering. Governors tended to side with them. In 1865, Governor Eyre suppressed a local uprising by the brutal use of martial law in a way that shocked most (but not all) Liberals at home (Semmel 1962). Assembly rule was terminated and Jamaica became a Crown colony ruled direct from London. This was an admission that social relations were too bitter and divided for liberal politics to stand any chance locally.

From a liberal perspective, India was hardly much better. In the eighteenth century it became notorious as the greatest fount of "old corruption". Men went out to get rich quickly, by exploiting native resources, before the climate damaged their health. Rapid British expansion gave enormous power to the East India Company, a part-trading, part-military operation. Family connections mattered greatly. The most famous attack on the malpractice of its leading men, the opposition Whigs' impeachment in 1787 of the former governor-general, Warren Hastings, was unsuccessful. The Indians who mattered were the princes; there was no representative politics. Reform seemed impossible; many people feared that British politics would be poisoned if governments at home were given the increased patronage and financial powers that came with direct rule over India. Only the shock of the 1857 Rebellion made direct rule possible, but the intensely racialized media reaction to the violence of that rebellion added to existing doubts about the viability of representative politics for India. For generations to come, Britain's priority there remained order and control.

In such a situation, there was little scope for "liberalism". When Liberal governments were in power, however, there was a discernible if cautious direction of travel after 1857. Liberal secretaries of state and viceroys wanted to cut taxes on Indian income, keep military spending low and avoid expansion on the northwest frontier. In the 1860s and 1870s, Secretary Wood and Viceroy Northbrook did something to protect Indian cotton planters, and Indian government revenue, from Lancashire competition. In the 1880s, Viceroy Ripon, anxious to prevent civil unrest, gave the tenants of Bengal more legal protection. Northbrook defended Indian press freedom as an essential conduit for public opinion given the lack of representative institutions (Moulton 1968: 268–71). Ripon stirred up controversy by proposing that native magistrates should exercise jurisdiction over Europeans. Wood in 1861, Ripon in the 1880s and Morley in 1909 all reformed Indian councils to strengthen indigenous representation. In 1917, Secretary Montagu was particularly anxious to reach out to Nationalists and acknowledge the Indian war effort. The 1919 Montagu–Chelmsford reforms devolved some second-order powers to provincial and local governments in which elected Indian administrators could exercise influence.

Most of the time, most British Liberals, like the public, preferred to ignore Indian misgovernment. However, some campaigned for Britain to accept more responsibility for it, especially from the 1850s. In writings such as *How Wars Are Got Up in India* (1853), Cobden charged that its garrisons and elaborate bureaucracy amounted to an enormous drain on Indian resources, and that it was in the career interest of local officials and military commanders to enlarge that drain by provoking conflicts with natives and seizing new territory. The India Reform Society attacked unaccountable Indian officialdom, "the creatures of the desk, and the creatures of favour" (Dickinson 1853: 13, 20). In the late 1880s, the MP Charles Bradlaugh was known as "The Member for India" because he became the main lobbyist for the newly formed Indian National Congress movement.

"Old corruption" arguments now re-emerged in a new form, because from the 1850s the state was anxious to build up the transport infrastructure necessary to secure control in India. It guaranteed that investors in loans to Indian railway companies would receive good interest rates, so they flooded in. James Geddes complained that this guarantee was a new form of British greed at India's expense, because it protected British investors at the expense of Indian economic development and native living standards. Lancashire cotton imports further unbalanced the economy. So soil was overcropped, leading to famine (Claeys 2010: 66–9). In response to the south Indian famine of the 1870s, William Digby, editor of the *Madras Times*, took up this argument and launched a major relief fund. When he returned to England, Digby became, in 1882, the first secretary of the new Liberal Party forum, the National Liberal Club. He secured the election of Dadabhai Naoroji as a member in 1885. Naoroji, a Liberal MP in the 1890s, became the most visible promoter of the argument that Indians were being impoverished and often starved by powerful vested interests, and that these could be rooted out only by increasing indigenous representation.

These arguments about the damage done to India by economic forces therefore dovetailed with those of J. A. Hobson's *Imperialism* (1902), the most famous Liberal critique of empire as a nest of greedy lobbies that promoted territorial expansion for their own selfish ends, unbalancing the working of the free market by requiring extra spending and taxes on defence and war, which then depressed domestic demand. Hobson's book was a response to the Boer War of 1899–1902, which became the most awkward of all imperial issues for the Liberal Party.

When it acquired the Cape of Good Hope from the Dutch in 1814, Britain thought that it was just getting an invaluable naval station. British settlers started to arrive; should the taxpayer protect them? The relentless expansion of responsibility after then was driven partly by Britons in the eastern Cape, but mostly by the inland treks of the Dutch Boers and their brutal attacks on the indigenous tribes in order to take their land. An argument emerged that the British government had a duty to hold the ring between the warring groups. In 1854, this argument seemed to have been lost: cost-cutting MPs persuaded the government to reverse its previous annexation of lands beyond the Orange River. In the 1870s and 1880s, however, some Liberals, such as William Forster, revived old evangelical anti-slavery language to argue that Britain had a mission to intervene in Africa to save souls from slavers and to improve race relations. From 1877, the Conservative government claimed that this mission could be realized if Britain presided over a confederation of the South African settler provinces. It annexed the Boer territory of Transvaal, triggering an unsuccessful conflict. In 1881, Gladstone's government had to compromise by recognizing nominal British suzerainty over a semi-independent Transvaal. The imperialist media climate of the 1880s and 1890s then pushed Liberals onto the defensive, while financial interests, symbolized by Cecil Rhodes and his fellow mining magnates or "randlords", were intensely keen to profit from the major gold discoveries of the 1890s and to take more territory for Britain. Hobson's critique was founded on his view that this capitalist pressure underlay the Conservative policy of 1895–9 to undermine Transvaal's self-governance, which resulted in war between Britain and the Boers.

The 1900 election was fought in the middle of the war. Conservatives claimed that "[e]very seat lost to the government is a seat gained to the Boers". The war divided Liberals badly – but they had always found South Africa an impossibly vexed question. This was partly because Forsterite evangelicalism clashed with the traditional radical desire to leave the country alone to save taxpayer money. Some Liberals felt that the Boers' expansion could not be stopped because their technological superiority over the indigenous tribes seemed a fact of life. Many argued on political grounds and upheld the principle of self-government, admiring the Boers' vigorous self-reliance and refusal to be bullied: Lloyd George described the government of the Orange Free State as "probably the best in the world" (Jones 1951: 27). There was also widespread detestation of randlord greed and dishonesty.

Asquith's Liberal government was then handed the problem of settling South African government after the Boer War. Its fundamental principle was that heavy-handed intervention from London must be avoided at all costs because it would destroy fragile British–Boer relations. Permanent peace and union in South Africa could be achieved only by conceding self-government to the Boer provinces and then trusting to local negotiation between their representatives and those of the Cape and Natal. So the London government was immensely relieved by their agreement to create a Union of South Africa in 1910. But this meant giving the politicians of the four provinces the power to make their own constitution. The Boers operated a colour bar in their provincial franchises; they now forced an agreement that only those of European descent should sit in the united parliament. Asquith admitted that opinion in Britain was "almost unanimous" that it was "invidious" to launch a new representative body on such a basis, but he argued that there was no alternative, given the need to respect "self-government" on prudential and principled grounds. He was reduced to making two points: first, that a united South African parliament was more likely to look after indigenous interests than separate Boer provinces would, because of the tradition of liberalism in Cape Province (where a multiracial franchise survived); second, that renewed British interference on behalf of the tribes would increase local hostility to them. Liberals, he concluded, must have faith in the idea that "the community itself, . . . which will benefit by improvement, which will suffer by deterioration" would come to see how it should adjust its representative institutions (Hansard 16 August 1909: 1008–14). This moment of liberal awakening never came. An element of remorse might be detected in British Liberals' subsequent enthusiasm for the anti-apartheid movement in the 1960s.

As Asquith's speech suggested, "self-government" had by now become the main Liberal principle for dealing with British colonies of European settlement. But the process by which this occurred was not straightforward. It was worked out gradually, first in Canada. The Liberal governments of the 1830s inherited from the Tories an unstable situation in the provinces of Upper and Lower Canada, and initially made it worse by policy drift. Lower Canada, around Quebec and Montreal, was primarily French-speaking, and resented the British; Upper Canada, around Toronto, primarily English-speaking, resented the power of English governors and flirted with pro-American secessionist talk. In 1837, there were revolts in both provinces. Rescuing the situation became a priority for the British cabinet. Russell managed the situation at home, while the cabinet sent two of its former colleagues to govern Canada in succession: the earl of Durham and Charles Poulett Thomson, Lord Sydenham. The aim was to shape and direct local politics. Both Durham and Sydenham had radical credentials – Sydenham had been MP for Manchester – and a belief that bold political leadership would gain popular confidence (Buckner 1985).

Their strategy involved a union of the two provinces on dignified terms that gave the minority French full representation but rested on (a correct) confidence that the faster-growing and commercially dynamic English community would dominate in future. It involved active leadership by the governor to make politicians of both nationalities compromise, minimizing sectarian division. And it involved a more efficient use of revenues, including a loan from the British state to reduce Upper Canada's crippling debt and to build infrastructure. Durham and Sydenham argued that Canada needed the sort of active politics enjoyed by the United States, where state governments relied on their popular standing and tax base to borrow money for the transport network and schools that would develop natural riches and secure communal progress. The loan was paid back by 1849, and once politics stabilized in the 1850s, banks on both sides of the Atlantic were keen to lend more.

Sydenham's vision of Canadian politics presupposed a strong liberal governor such as himself, rather than sectarian political parties competing for power. After he died, however, they developed quickly, and when the Liberals returned to power in Britain in 1846, it was clear to the Colonial Secretary Earl Grey and his Canadian governor, Lord Elgin, that Britain had to grant Canada "responsible government", that is, surrender by the Crown of control of policy and patronage to the leaders of whichever party had a majority in the legislature. Elgin's policy was to accept whatever coalitions and policies could command a majority, but in a high-profile way that stressed the governor's continuing importance for effective political cooperation. Specifically, he encouraged coalitions that included French as well as British representatives, accepted the proposal to reinstitute French as a second official language and supported the contentious measure of 1849 that legalized compensation to French Canadians whose property had been destroyed by the army during the 1837 rebellion (Buckner 1985). The parties, in turn, accepted the formal supremacy of the governor and the Crown-in-parliament system of government. Grey and Elgin felt that they had maintained the constitution against pressure for republicanism and annexation to the United States.

However, the unstoppable drift towards "responsible government" in Canada encouraged settlers in the other colonies, and backbench MPs in the British parliament, to feel that this was the natural solution for all colonies of free-born Britons. In New Zealand and Australia, settlers complained about Colonial Office dictation. In Britain, economizing radicals resented the amount spent on colonial office-holders, especially in the financial crisis and economic depression of 1847–8. Many of them thought that, after the free trade revolution of the 1840s, there was no need for expensive imperial governance at all. In 1849, the Society for the Reform of Colonial Government was set up to promote self-government. Some Peelite Tories had links with settler colonies as well, and between 1853 and 1855, the Peelite colonial secretary, the Duke of Newcastle, ceded "responsible government" to New Zealand and to the more developed Australian colonies. Ministries resting on assembly majorities were from now on given effective power. This was not because of a great increase of pressure from those colonies; it was because this new British government, and parliament, found it politically appealing to identify with an image of the British world as a communion of free peoples (Parry 2024: 253–5).

However, this new norm for settler colonies required the British government to surrender its responsibility for native protection, which appalled some Whiggish and evangelical Liberals. (Something of their alternative approach can be seen in the 1853 constitution for the Cape, which rejected full "responsible government" and brought in a multi-racial franchise, in the hope of settling British–native conflicts by amicable political discussion.) Grey had opposed the idea of responsible government for New Zealand when colonial secretary, because he feared that the white settlers would oppress the Maori and steal their land. When he left office in 1852, the draft constitution he left for his successor was careful to reserve land purchase and Maori policy to the Crown, as well as to acknowledge the continuing applicability of Maori law in their districts. By the 1860s, however, this vision of slow and harmonious improvement in New Zealand had collapsed. Grey blamed the cession of responsible government in 1854–5 and the subsequent pressure imposed on governors by the increasing number of European settlers. The latter gained control over revenue. The reservation of native policy to the governor became nominal. Settler pressure ruled everything. School and hospital building for the Maori stopped. They lost their political representation. The Maori war of 1860–61 began when settlers demanded seizure of a piece of land on terms that the chiefs disputed (Parry 2024: 255–6).

As the case of New Zealand showed, most governors were unable to play the wise leadership role, disciplining settlers' biases, that Grey envisaged. Settlers were able to skew land and franchise policy to their benefit, and could also lobby Westminster MPs. This land grab was justified by the Enlightenment language of improvement, but the driving forces behind it were clearly the economic interests and insecurities, and the racism, of planters, settlers and merchants. Racial oppression in New Zealand and elsewhere was not the result of "liberalism", except that it followed naturally from the concession of representative politics.

So Liberals voiced a great variety of opinions on Britain's relations with its sprawling empire. One school of thought wanted nothing to do with it, seeing it as a hive of unpleasant adventurers on the make, costing the taxpayer money and damaging Britain's reputation. Others believed that, in the self-governing settler colonies, empire, defined as an expression of British self-reliance and entrepreneurship, showed the national character in good light and cost the taxpayer pleasingly little. In *The Expansion of England* (1883), the Liberal historian J. R. Seeley acknowledged the errors of past generations of greedy adventurers, especially in India, but believed that the task of the next cohort of public-spirited administrators was to try to atone for that. Some Liberal imperial politicians found a career articulating the benefits that fair-minded British rule could bring. The Earl of Dufferin, for example, who was sent to Egypt in 1883 to justify the British intervention of 1882, produced an uplifting and patriotic report arguing that Britain stood a better chance than the Ottomans or any other power of restoring peace to a troubled land and improving the condition of the fellahin, and at any rate that it had the responsibility to try (Gailey 2016: 188–94).

The imperial policy of Liberal governments was profoundly constrained by the weight of the legacy they inherited across the world, by settlers' clamour for protection and by the small room for manoeuvre they faced in the light of growing Conservative and media jingoism. In New Zealand and South Africa, and to some extent in Australia and Canada, it was also constrained by the juggernaut of representative politics itself, as settler democracy produced a stridently racialist white culture but left little scope for intervention to curb it by British Liberals, even had they agreed on what they thought about it.

PART II

Since 1914

4

A centre party in a two-party system

The Liberal Party lost its dominant place in British politics during the First World War and has suffered from two interlinked problems ever since. First, it has been a squeezed third party in a first-past-the-post electoral system, in which elections have been a competition for office between the Conservative and Labour parties. Second, national political debate came to focus on central government policies towards the economy, especially Labour's interventionist economic plans, which Conservatives painted as "socialism". In a debate on that issue, Liberals were at a strong disadvantage (as the other parties intended), since their arguments were not as simplistic and memorable as those of their competitors. Liberals did not want to reduce politics to an ideological battleground between capital and labour and between free enterprise and state intervention. As a result, they seemed irrelevant to the big economic debates that the media regarded as central to politics. This further cemented their third-party status, which in turn led them to call for proportional representation (PR). Liberals argued that PR was needed to prevent the economy being damaged by a succession of single-party governments alternating between two clashing and simplistic economic philosophies.

In the early 1960s, the Liberal Party began to revive. The idea of a free-thinking centre party liberated from the narrow approaches of its two opponents began to resonate with voters looking for a different politics. From the late 1970s, this revival gathered pace, as the party, and its successor the Liberal Democrats (Lib Dems), benefited from the perception that both main parties were too extremist, together with class dealignment in voting patterns. But since the 1990s, Conservative and Labour governments have taken a broadly social market approach to economic management, so Lib Dems have no longer had a distinctively centrist stance on economics. Instead, this chapter argues that Lib

Dem economic policy statements have usually had *political* purposes: to focus attention on a particular political cause, to attack concentrations of power or to promote party realignment.

Despite the narrowing of economic ground between the political parties, they have still suffered when opponents can portray them as in hock to vested interests. At times, Labour has seemed beholden either to the unions or (as under Jeremy Corbyn in 2015–19) to "socialist" ideology. In office, the Conservatives have been accused of prioritizing the interests of the wealthy over those of ordinary voters: the few rather than the many, in the old slogan that was resuscitated to attack them in the 1990s. The Lib Dems have benefited from this latter argument as well as Labour, because they have collected the votes of disgruntled voters in relatively affluent constituencies who have become disillusioned with the performance of Conservative governments, on the economy, on public services or recently on Europe. This trend was first observed in 1964 and 1974 and became even more evident in 1997, as the Lib Dems honed their electoral machine more ruthlessly, and in 2024.

Political marginalization, 1915–45

Between 1915 and 1924, the Liberal Party underwent an extraordinary decline. If there had been an election in 1915, it would have expected to win it, but at the poll of 1924 it collected only 40 of the 615 seats in parliament. The fundamental cause of this change was the revolution in British political culture during the First World War. Until the 1910s, the main topics of political debate had been nineteenth-century staples: parliamentary reform, the House of Lords, the land, the Church, Ireland and tariffs. By 1922, the franchise, Welsh Church and Irish issues were virtually settled, and the House of Lords was much more cautious about blocking democratically sanctioned legislation. The overwhelmingly important question was social reconstruction and stability after the war. One rallying cry was better homes for soldier heroes. The Russian Revolution indicated the risks of not pacifying the large, active and well-organized male working class that was fully enfranchised in 1918. The wartime state greatly expanded its control over industry, encouraging the Labour Party to advocate public control of the means of production, distribution and exchange. Trade union membership rose from 2.5 million in 1910 to 8.3 million in 1920, as unions benefited from wartime shortages and lobbied effectively for better pay, job security and working conditions. To pay for the war, the basic rate of income tax rose from 9d in 1914 to 6s in 1918. Would middle-class voters accept this in peacetime?

Between 1918 and 1926, governments had to manage major strikes, labour lockouts, inflationary risks and intense discussions about the role of the state in the peacetime economy. In 1918, the Labour Party won over 20 per cent of the vote and in 1922 nearly 30 per cent. Tensions between capital and labour dominated politics: business versus the unions, capitalism versus socialism, tax cuts versus investment in national renewal. To focus on these tensions benefited both the Conservative and Labour parties: the former suggested that unions and "socialism" were dangerous and unpatriotic, while the latter implied the same about greedy capitalist bosses. Both wanted to marginalize the Liberal Party and attract its supporters. It was vulnerable prey, because it was suffering from a paralysing split between its two leading men.

In the first two years of the war, Asquith and Lloyd George were supremely confident and powerful politicians. Asquith had been prime minister for well over eight years by the autumn of 1916. He had defeated Joseph Chamberlain and the case for tariffs, and Conservative leader Arthur Balfour and the House of Lords; he expected soon to do the same to Wilhelm II and Germany. When Lloyd George organized a successful move against him in December 1916, the Welshman had himself been a high-ranking cabinet minister for 11 years. He had revolutionized financial and social policy and had become arguably the most effective modernizing force in British history; why should he not succeed in running the war more efficiently? Asquith was only 64, Lloyd George 53. Both were exceptionally able lawyers, processors of policy and public speakers. Lloyd George's coup was mounted with the support of key Conservative ministers: the government had been reconstituted as a wartime coalition in May 1915. Although Asquith was undoubtedly drained by the enormous responsibilities of war management, he continued to resent his removal from the premiership, especially as he remained Liberal Party leader while Lloyd George increasingly relied on Conservative MPs to buttress his position as prime minister.

The die was cast at the 1918 election, when Lloyd George arranged for candidates supporting his coalition government to receive a coupon guaranteeing that they would be unopposed by other coalition parties. As a result, 127 Liberals were returned with the coupon and only 36 without it, while the Conservatives dominated parliament with 379 seats. Asquith lost his seat, but the 27 Liberal MPs who remained outside the coalition still regarded him as their leader; he returned at the Paisley by-election in 1920. They felt that Lloyd George had betrayed the party in pursuit of untrammelled power resting on his temporary popularity as the man who had won the war. They also complained at the brutal and illiberal repression being carried out by British soldiers in Ireland.

Impatient with the constraints of party, Lloyd George brought several no-nonsense businessmen, such as Sir Eric Geddes, into government. Capitalists also provided him with funds for his supporters' election contests. He built up a "Political Fund" which was eventually worth £3–4 million, much of it derived from the sale of honours to wealthy arrivistes: a knighthood was said to cost £10,000 and a peerage £50,000. The 1922 Birthday Honours list created a particular scandal (Searle 1987). Asquithians berated the return to "old corruption" and cultivated an image of moral superiority, although Asquith's pre-war government had itself faced allegations about sales of honours. His "Holy Family" of lieutenants and protectors made his style of Liberalism look arrogant, supercilious and limited, rather than the effective and pragmatic force that he had led from 1908 to 1914.

Lloyd George hoped to reconstruct politics around a modernizing quasi-presidential approach. He was undermined, partly by his ego and volatility, but above all by the reviving confidence of the Conservative Party, which soon had no reason to endure subordination to him. Lloyd George may have expected the Conservatives to split over the enhanced role for the state in housing and welfare that his government proposed. Instead, Conservative and taxpayer hostility to major social spending forced the government to scale it back in 1921: it reduced income tax, cut the subsidies for new housing, and set up the Geddes Committee, which in 1922 urged a large-scale reduction of public sector services and salaries. The Tories then pulled the plug on Lloyd George's premiership. By this time, Lloyd George had lost most of his progressive credentials, and after the 1922 election Labour became the main opposition to the new Conservative government. Several Liberal MPs – E. D. Morel, C. P. Trevelyan, Arthur Ponsonby, Noel Buxton, Josiah Wedgwood – had already joined Labour during or immediately after the war.

In 1923, the Conservative Party leader Stanley Baldwin sought an electoral mandate for the introduction of tariffs. This allowed Asquithians and Lloyd Georgeites to patch up their differences, defending free trade against a common enemy. But the Liberal Party was still unable to control the direction of politics. After the 1923 election, the Conservatives lacked a majority, while there were 191 Labour MPs and only 158 Liberals. Asquith decided that the Labour leader Ramsay MacDonald should be allowed to form a government, since he was the leader of the free trade party with most MPs. Liberal Party history made it difficult to resist Labour's claims that in some way it represented "the people". If Asquith thought that MacDonald in government would defer to his status as elder statesman and kingmaker, he was deluded. It was not just that MacDonald, like Asquith, did not want a formal Lib–Lab coalition; MacDonald now saw that he could destroy the Liberal threat and make Liberal MPs and voters see that Labour was the more logical choice in future (Bentley 1974: 56–7). The new Labour cabinet gained respectability from the presence of several Liberal defectors with government experience, such as Trevelyan and Lord Haldane. Haldane left his butler to deal with the press scrimmage outside his house while he negotiated his acceptance of the Lord Chancellorship.

After ten months of minority Labour government, the Liberals were the main losers at the 1924 election. They lacked money and won only 40 seats; Asquith was defeated and had to retreat to the Lords. Many middle-class Liberal voters switched to the Conservatives, horrified by the idea of more Liberal-aided "socialism". This anti-socialist mood was shared by some former Liberal MPs, including Winston Churchill who, from a mixture of ambition and ideological preference, had abandoned the party after being defeated at Dundee in 1922. He now returned as Chancellor of the Exchequer in Baldwin's Conservative government. Other leading Liberals – Hamar Greenwood, Alfred Mond, Hilton Young – defected to the Conservatives as the 1920s wore on. They disliked not only Labour's connections with striking unions but also Lloyd George's restless and unsuccessful attempts to regain the political initiative, which began with an attempt to refloat his land campaign in 1925. The General Strike of 1926 was a catalyst for severe rows within the party: Lloyd George was appalled by the hostility of many Liberals towards it. Shortly after it, Asquith's stroke finally ended his political career, and Lloyd George could no longer be denied the leadership.

Lloyd George used his accumulated political funds to galvanize Liberal thinkers who had been looking for solutions to Britain's severe industrial malaise. Under the auspices of the party's think tank, the Liberal Summer School, a Liberal Industrial Inquiry was established to investigate five aspects of the industrial economy, chaired by John Maynard Keynes, Ramsay Muir, Ernest Simon, Lloyd George and E. H. Gilpin. In 1928 it produced a 500-page report, called *Britain's Industrial Future*, but popularly dubbed the *Yellow Book*. The report refuted the assumption that the economy needed simplistic dogma, whether individualism or socialism. It urged instead more effective state supervision of industrial monopolies and the Bank of England, a council of industry charged with maintaining good relations between employers and employees and a national investment board to superintend a programme of public works, especially on roads and housing. This public works scheme was popularized in March 1929 in a policy document launched by Lloyd George, *We Can Conquer Unemployment*.

The Yellow Book was a coherent statement of mostly familiar themes. Already at the 1924 election, Asquith had called for public credit to be spent on national development works such as power supply and afforestation, to give work to the unemployed; this itself built on the principle of the 1909 Development Fund (see page 63). The *Book*'s loan-financed programme of public works was presented as an emergency strategy to stimulate the economy, not as part of a general economic theory. Its significance lay less in its economic vision than in its political assertiveness. Lloyd George and Keynes insisted that the key to Liberal politics was the tapping of moralized energy: that politicians had a responsibility to address the causes of strikes and underinvestment, and that by doing so with bold charisma they would boost business confidence to invest, and voter confidence in democracy.

The Liberals mounted a modest revival in 1929, but the polarized climate remained their enemy: their share of the vote in three-cornered contests fell, and their 59 seats were only enough to defeat the Conservative government and install another minority Labour government. Then in 1930–31 a severe economic downturn created a large government spending deficit; bankers urged welfare cuts as a prerequisite of new loans. The decision of MacDonald's Labour government to reduce unemployment benefit by 10 per cent in August 1931 split the Labour Party badly and led to the fall of the government. It was replaced by a coalition National Government under MacDonald but dominated by Conservatives.

In the long term, the crisis of 1931 damaged the Liberals even more than it did Labour. There had already been tensions in 1930 between Lloyd George and the barrister John Simon, who many saw as Asquith's successor, over whether the party should form a pact with Labour. In 1926, Simon had claimed that the General Strike was illegal; from 1929, he owed his seat at Spen Valley to a pact with the Conservatives. Simon resigned the party whip in June 1931. A strong middle group of Liberal MPs disliked the bankers' narrow focus on unemployment benefit cuts and urged instead a broader national treaty under which all classes would make economic sacrifices. However, MacDonald thought this was impractical. Except for the ill Lloyd George, the leading Liberal MPs joined the National Government, to uphold the principle of responsible balanced budgets. It seemed the patriotic thing to do; it appealed to their instinctive anti-socialism. The economic climate now seemed too dire for a modestly counter-cyclical public works programme, making retrenchment the only, disagreeable, alternative (Sloman 2015: 77–8).

It quickly became clear that most Conservatives demanded another remedy: import duties, in response to the erection of tariff walls by other countries. Free trade remained a fundamental historic principle for most Liberals; their instinctive anti-Toryism rested on it. But given the damage done by cheap foreign goods, others felt that free trade was an outdated concept. Keynes himself now advocated tariffs. The MP Leslie Hore-Belisha called it an old shibboleth, like freedom of contract, which Liberals had abandoned long before (Dutton 2007: 223). Hore-Belisha joined Simon in forming a separate Liberal National group in October 1931, pledging to support the National Government even if it introduced protection. Herbert Samuel, who emerged as Liberal leader in place of Lloyd George, and home secretary in the National Government, appreciated that the party would be destroyed at the upcoming election if it left the government. So he agreed that protection should remain an open issue among ministers. On this basis, 72 Liberal MPs were returned at the 1931 election, almost equally split between Samuelites and Simonites (and Lloyd George's separate small family group). An import duty was quickly agreed, and Samuel was persuaded to remain home secretary on its introduction in early 1932. Later in the year, however, the Samuelites resigned when the government signed up to a system of imperial preference negotiated at Ottawa.

Simon's Liberal Nationals argued that the defence of sound finance and hostility to sectional socialism trumped historic Liberal free trade principles. Moreover, since the shrunken Liberal Party was unlikely ever to form a government on its own, the way to "Be an Effective Liberal" was by working with other politicians in coalitions (Dutton 2007: 224). They remained a separate group, who argued that their presence in government through the 1930s helped Baldwin to marginalize the Tory right. Simon collected four high offices of state as a result; many Liberals criticized his failure to stand up to Japan as foreign secretary in 1932–3. Liberal National MPs become reliant on pacts with local Conservative parties to retain their seats. Attempts at reunification between the two Liberal groupings in 1944–6 broke down over the question of cooperation with the postwar Conservative opposition. From 1947, the Liberal Nationals (renamed National Liberals), now led by John Maclay, were formally allied with the Conservative Party. They returned between 17 and 21 MPs in each of the four elections of the 1950s and finally disappeared as a separate body in 1968. In the early 1960s, their candidates included future Conservative cabinet ministers Ian Gilmour and John Nott.

The survival of the National Government through the 1930s meant that the mainstream Liberal Party, in opposition to it, could not find a sense of purpose. Free trade was no longer a powerful moral cause embodying hostility to vested interests but a technical question.

Archibald Sinclair, Liberal leader from 1935, cooperated with Churchill against appeasement and was included in his wartime coalition cabinet from 1940. Meanwhile, Liberal activists shared in the discussions about postwar reconstruction and the general revival of interest in state intervention. The 1943 Party Assembly adopted a series of reports on postwar policy; it revived the *Yellow Book*'s proposals for counter-cyclical public works, a national development plan and trade boards. In February 1945, the Assembly adopted the principle of full employment that William Beveridge had publicized in his report of November 1944. It was seen as a natural corollary of his very popular proposals of 1942 for a national social insurance scheme. Beveridge had had a distinguished career as a civil servant and as director of the London School of Economics, and the success of his social insurance report prompted him to seek a parliamentary seat. Persuaded by his friend Violet Bonham Carter (Asquith's daughter), it was as a Liberal that he became MP for Berwick-on-Tweed in 1944.

Beveridge fitted well into the party because his social insurance ideas followed naturally from the principles of the 1911 reforms. They rested on compulsory contributions from employers, workers and the state, which were to be accompanied by a public assistance safety net for those who had not made the necessary contributions. State social insurance would give the insured worker a guaranteed minimum level of support: he would aim to top it up by voluntary provision, and therefore develop self-reliance. Like other Edwardian-era New Liberals, Beveridge hoped that this scheme would correct tendencies to underconsumptionism in the national economy. But he had also developed an interest in the more dirigiste arguments that Keynes had set out in his *General Theory* of 1936: that vigorous state planning might be necessary to correct economic instability and secure full employment (Sloman 2015: 149–56).

The party Assembly adopted the Beveridge reports with pride, and Elliott Dodds, a well-known sceptic about state intervention in the economy, seconded the resolution on full employment, justifying it on libertarian principles (Sloman 2015: 154–5). At the 1945 election, Liberals made a great deal of Beveridge's adhesion to the party, but they combined their support for social security and full employment with attacks on "socialism" and a cautious line on nationalization. They needed to differentiate themselves from the Labour Party even while presenting themselves as sympathetic to postwar regeneration.

In truth, however, the Liberals were irrelevant to the outcome in 1945. Public desperation for a new politics was channelled into support for the main opposition, the Labour Party. The consensus over Beveridge's plans was so strong that his own party affiliation was immaterial. The Liberal Party returned just 12 MPs, overwhelmingly from rural areas, including seven from Wales, where memories of battles against Tory landowners still meant something. Sinclair and Beveridge were defeated.

Modern two-party politics seemed to have superseded the Liberal Party, but this was partly because both main parties were drawing significantly on its history and traditions. At any point between 1935 and 1955, many more MPs were ex-Liberals than current ones. As Keynes observed as early as 1925: "Possibly the Liberal Party cannot serve the State in any better way than by supplying Conservative Governments with Cabinets, and Labour Governments with ideas" (Keynes 1931: 343).

The Liberal Party and economic politics, 1945–88

After the war, the Liberal Party's fundamental problems remained. General elections under the first-past-the-post system continued to be a contest for power between the two big parties. Unlike those parties, the Liberals were not identified either with business or with labour, and until the 1990s British politics turned fundamentally on the organization of the industrial economy and the role of the trade unions. Voters often told Liberal canvassers that the party had no policies (Howarth 2014: 25). This was not true. Its core approach was what has been called liberal Keynesianism: a reliance on adjusting fiscal and monetary policy to check unemployment and inflation (Sloman 2015: 167–8). After the war, however, this ceased to be unusual. More distinctively, the party consistently advocated schemes for democracy, co-ownership and joint policy-making in the workplace, in the hope of smoothing industrial tensions but also of spreading the principle of private ownership (through profit-sharing and company share schemes). What voters found puzzling was Liberal determination not to be identified with a major economic interest.

In these decades, periodic variations from, or embellishments of, the party's core centrist position were determined by two factors. The first was personalities, as was inevitable once the parliamentary party shrunk to single figures: it won only nine seats in 1950 and six in 1951. In 1950, the party leader, Clement Davies, told Gilbert Murray that there was really no party, just a number of individuals with "completely divergent views" (Sloman 2015: 167). The party tended to attract combative characters with idiosyncratic opinions and large egos. One such, Oliver Smedley, developed a following at party assemblies in the early 1950s by arguing for a purist consumerist free market approach. He stood in the constituency of the leading Conservative R. A. Butler on the historic cry of free trade against agricultural protection. In 1953, he tried to get the party to reject guaranteed prices for agricultural products, but was defeated by a Radical Reform group of pragmatic university graduates (Sloman 2015: 195–201).

The second was changes in political fashion. Liberals' brief wartime enthusiasm for planning did not survive the experience of Labour government after 1945. After the coal industry was dealt with, Liberals lost any interest in further nationalization: Davies complained that "everything is being organised from the centre" (Dutton 2012: 142–3). They also urged retrenchment. Their instinctive hostility to socialism was reflected in pacts with the Conservatives to share the representation of the two seats in Huddersfield in 1950, giving each party a free run against Labour in one of the seats. This practice was extended to Bolton in 1951. Huddersfield was a symbolic site for such an arrangement because it was the base of Elliott Dodds, the editor of a local newspaper and prominent Liberal activist and Nonconformist layman. Dodds became the most effective proponent of an economic libertarianism that was more nuanced than Smedley's. It was based on the principle of distributism: the extension of property ownership to all as a means of boosting growth and democratic participation while checking state bureaucracy. Dodds became chairman of the Unservile State Group in 1953. In the group's signature volume, Dodds argued that in a Liberal society "the release and stimulation of private endeavour and voluntary agencies of service and mutual aid [will] diminish the rôle of the State" (Watson 1957: 19).

These pacts also revealed the precariousness of the Liberals' position. Barely 100 Liberal candidates contested the general elections of 1951 and 1955. Membership, central income and representation on local councils all hit lows in the early 1950s. Churchill's Conservative Party defeated Attlee's Labour government at the 1951 election despite not winning the popular vote, because the Liberal vote collapsed from 9.1 to 2.5 per cent, and almost two-thirds of it went to Conservatives, with a particular effect in marginal seats (Butler 1952: 271). Churchill courted these voters, boasting of his own role in the pre-war Liberal governments. He wooed the Liberal leader Clement Davies, and his old friend Violet Bonham Carter, with the offer of government posts after the 1951 election. Davies rejected the offer and Bonham Carter failed to win election at Colne Valley; otherwise the party might easily have disappeared. Even so, five of the six Liberal MPs returned at the 1955 election were unopposed by Conservative candidates. The distinctiveness of Dodds's distributism also declined. During the 1950s, the Conservative Party pursued an extensive programme of private house-building and reaped the rewards among aspirational voters.

Most Liberal activists disliked the Conservative pacts. The task of Jo Grimond, who succeeded Clement Davies as the party's leader in 1956, was to rework its image into something more uplifting and distinctive. Grimond respected deeply the ideals of community self-help that he found in his Orkney and Shetland constituency; he remained viscerally hostile to the dead hand of bureaucratic socialism (as became particularly clear in his writings from the late 1970s). Yet he found a way to revitalize the party's image and thinking, through his charisma, interest in ideas and ability to communicate on television. He made the Liberal Party again what Lloyd George and Keynes had wanted in the 1920s, a movement that could attract enthusiasts through its dynamism, intellectual vibrancy and moral seriousness.

Lord Beveridge (left) talks with Jo Grimond (centre) and Frank Byers (right), the Party's candidate for Bolton East, at a reception given at Eastbourne, on the eve of the Liberal Party's annual assembly in September 1960

Source: PA Images/Alamy Stock Photo.

Grimond aimed to harness widespread intelligentsia dislike of sterile two-party political argument. He held both parties responsible for Britain's postwar economic stagnation, claiming that competitiveness and growth prospects were being harmed by their extreme positions and particularly their complacency about the damage done by the monopoly power of big businesses and trade unions. If Britain was to address its changed position in the postwar world, fresh thinking and a rational pragmatism were needed, rejecting the tired language of class war. This approach struck chords with a new generation of activists, especially university graduates: party membership rose from 76,000 in 1953 to 351,000 in 1963 (Sloman 2015: 204).

The new image was boosted by enthusiasm for policy and research. In 1961 and 1962, Grimond encouraged Harry Cowie, the party's director of research, and other young Liberals to produce a series of pamphlets for the party conferences, about competition, consumer protection, economic planning and the promotion of growth. They emphasized increased investment, particularly a ten-year plan for education and school-building, as well as membership of the Common Market. In 1964, Liberals proposed a social security tax to address the inadequacies of the Beveridge settlement.

This blitz of policy proposals represented a skilful political readjustment rather than a new philosophy about the role of the state. At the core of Grimond's thinking was active citizenship and political participation, which he envisaged as checking central bureaucratic power. In his 1959 volume, *The Liberal Future*, he imagined a Liberal society of self-reliant citizens earning good wages, in which the need for social services and state pensions might well disappear (Grimond 1959: 103). As the *Liberal News* masthead put it, the Liberals were "the only Progressive Non-Socialist party" (Sloman 2015: 208). Investment in infrastructure was presented as in the tradition of the *Yellow Book*. Competition and entrepreneurship were also praised. Grimond welcomed the Conservatives' plans for a National Economic Development Council, set out in 1961, on the grounds that private owners would benefit from a regime of constructive discussions between all sides in industry and an improved sense of national purpose. All the parties were responding to a shift in the language of debate about economic policy between 1958 and 1962, in Britain and the United States. Liberal Keynesianism had not reversed Britain's relative shortfall in economic growth; the Beveridge reforms had not abolished poverty; sociologists such as Michael Shanks argued that Britain was held back by its class divisions; J. K. Galbraith and other economists urged more coherent national planning. But Grimond himself remained sceptical about anything that smacked of bureaucratic planning and production targets. His idea of state intervention also prioritized the tackling of specific political grievances, hence his support for agricultural subsidies, and for loans and grants to help depressed regions such as the Scottish Highlands.

As explored in Chapter 5, Grimond led the party to urge entry to the Common Market, or European Economic Community (EEC). He defeated the purist Smedleyites, who opposed the EEC on account of its tariff walls. Liberal commitment to the Common Market further marginalized free market language within the party. When the party constitution was revised in 1969, the commitment to free trade disappeared from the preamble (Sloman 2015: 223). Smedley remained a zealous libertarian, went off to run a pirate radio station, and killed a rival operator who threatened him in his house (he was cleared of manslaughter).

Above all, Grimond's leadership aimed to make the Liberal Party matter in national politics. He tried to challenge the rigidities of the two-party system. He was responding to the rise of Anthony Crosland's revisionist socialism in the Labour Party, which focused not on public ownership but on public services, educational reform and social equality. By positioning Liberalism as a movement of modernization and new ideas, he hoped to widen the breach between Labour revisionists and the party's old guard after Labour's third successive election defeat in 1959. The prize might be a reorganization of the centre-left, with Liberal involvement. This positioning meant abandoning the pacts with Conservatives (with the result that the Bolton and Huddersfield seats were both lost in 1964), but Liberals hoped to challenge the Conservatives in other seats. They benefited from suburban voters' disillusionment at the Conservative government's economic record after 1959 and the rising cost of living. Liberal ratings in opinion polls after 1957 closely tracked the rate of inflation. This approach paid dividends with a sensational victory at the Orpington by-election of 1962, caused additionally by high mortgage rates squeezing homeowners. That boosted the party's media profile further.

This was the first of several increasingly powerful Liberal revivals building primarily on voter discontent with Conservative governments. In 1964, the Liberal share of the vote rose from 5.9 to 11.2 per cent; in February 1974 it rose further to 19.3 per cent (against 7.5 per cent in 1970). The 1970s have been seen as a "decade of dealignment", in which perceptions of social class identity became less important in determining voting patterns (Särlvik & Crewe 1983). But the Liberal Party was not just the passive recipient of such a shift: it worked hard to persuade voters that a class-based, two-party system was a major cause of Britain's economic malaise (Sloman 2022). In October 1974, it stood candidates in almost every seat in England and Wales, in a clear bid again to be a national party. Grimond's successor as party leader, Jeremy Thorpe, was a natural showman and orator, whose charisma, style and mimicry made him popular both on television and among party workers. In 1972–3, five by-election victories by mostly colourful Liberal candidates also boosted the party's publicity: the lugubrious radio panellist Clement Freud, who had starred in television dog food adverts with an equally hangdog bloodhound called Henry, won the Isle of Ely, shortly after Rochdale was gained by Cyril Smith, a larger-than-life, blunt northerner. (Both men were later accused of child sexual abuse, while Thorpe was tried at the Old Bailey on charges of conspiracy and incitement to murder.)

In the mid-1970s, Britain seemed in political and economic crisis, and the two elections of 1974 produced no clear winner: as a result, the Liberal Party mattered in national politics. In 1977–8, Thorpe's successor, David Steel, secured the party valuable political attention when he forged the Lib–Lab pact, which propped up the minority Labour government of James Callaghan for 18 months.

This self-presentation as the rational alternative to the politics of extremism, division and economic failure reached its apogee at the 1983 election. By this time, Margaret Thatcher had come to power, had presided over deep spending cuts, and was preparing for confrontation with the miners' union. Meanwhile the Labour Party had split badly over economic policy, with the Bennite left apparently on the verge of winning control. Four ex-cabinet ministers left Labour and set up the Social Democratic Party (SDP) in 1981. Twenty-eight Labour MPs eventually joined it. The Liberals and SDP formed an alliance, and at the 1983 election put forward a joint manifesto appealing to the public to "turn their backs on dogma and bitterness and [choose] a new road of partnership and progress". Thatcher offered neglect, Labour an ideology of rigid nationalization: both were "prisoners of ideology". The watchword of the SDP–Liberal Alliance, instead, was "co-operation: not just between our parties but between management and workers, between people of different races and above all between government and people". The message seemed perfectly pitched for an increasingly post-industrial electorate: the Alliance won 25.4 per cent of the vote, just 2 per cent less than Labour. This remains the second highest percentage of the vote ever achieved by a third party, behind only Asquith's 29.7 per cent in 1923.

The Liberal Democrats and economic politics

In 1988, the Liberals and SDP merged under a new leader, the Liberal Paddy Ashdown, and since 1989 have traded under the name Liberal Democrats. In the early 1980s, the polarized stances of the other parties seemed likely to make the Lib Dems' centrist economic policy attractively distinctive. Since then, the grounds of debate have narrowed, particularly once Tony Blair's New Labour faction developed a "Third Way" policy based on social market principles. Under Blair, and perhaps again under Keir Starmer, the Labour Party's language on economics is designed to occupy the political centre ground itself, stressing its pragmatism and fiscal discipline. In 1997, Blair and Gordon Brown accepted the spending targets of the previous Conservative government, and the introduction of private investment into public services.

This has given the Lib Dems major difficulties in creating a distinctive position on economic issues. Shortly after Blair became Labour leader, Ashdown ruefully reflected: "I have been building the Party to fill a certain gap in politics, which I know is there and which would give us real electoral appeal. But then along comes Blair with all the power of Labour behind him, and fills exactly the space I have been aiming at for the last seven years!" (Ashdown 2000: 273).

When the merger first took place, there was speculation that the new party would show distinct evidence of the intellectual influence of revisionist Labour economic thinking of the 1950s and 1960s: of social democracy. It was assumed that the SDP would continue the revisionists' managerial and centralizing approach to economic policy, in the hope of securing full employment. A small faction of Liberals opposed to merger, led by Michael Meadowcroft, was particularly opposed to Social Democrat planning culture, which Meadowcroft associated with "the vast expanse of soulless council house estates" built since the war (Dutton 2012: 225–6). Yet after the merger, these differences of culture hardly mattered within the new party. Most Social Democrats now advocated decentralization, and two high-profile SDP figures, Charles Kennedy and Robert Maclennan, felt that they had become Liberals in outlook (Ashdown 2001: 7). The merged party was originally called the Social and Liberal Democrats, but in 1989 the "Social and" was dropped from the new party's name. This was because it seemed too cumbersome, but the switch was nonetheless suggestive. The party's focus and ethos clearly remain "liberal", "democratic" and political, which necessarily limits its keenness on central economic management.

In 2004, the Lib Dems enjoyed a flurry of intellectual controversy when a group of provocateurs within the party published the *Orange Book*. The editors were two City financiers, David Laws and the hedge fund manager Paul Marshall, and the authors included the party's future leader, Nick Clegg. The title, a nod to the 1928 *Yellow Book*, boasted a desire to reset party priorities on economic policy in the light of the recognition by Blair's Labour Party as well as Conservatives that the market should help to provide public services. The editors claimed that Liberals should avoid "nanny-state liberalism" and should be bolder in embracing themes of choice, competition and consumer power (Laws & Marshall 2004: 24).

However, the *Orange Book*'s critics within the party pointed out that this was a fuss over very little: that these were already standard party themes, that all Liberals were suspicious of remote bureaucracies and that the "nanny state" was a straw woman (in fact a favourite trope of past generations of Liberal provocateurs, including William Harcourt in 1871 as well as Grimond). Duncan Brack, Richard Grayson and David Howarth showed that the book's attempt to set up a philosophical distance between classical and social Liberalism was inaccurate and retrograde. Classical Liberalism was not practical politics. All Liberals should recognize the merit of a pragmatic "social market" approach: Orange Bookers accepted that the state had some role in economic planning, while the market alone could not defeat major problems such as climate change. Private enterprise and the welfare state were both socially beneficial ideas; the challenge was how to apply each most effectively in specific situations (Brack, Grayson & Howarth 2007; Hickson 2009: 43–9). Paddy Ashdown had already worked to distance the party from "soggy corporatism" in the 1990s. He had expressed his admiration for competition, small businesses and enterprise, and criticized the tendency of public services to be run in the interests of those who worked there: "the producer interest" (Ashdown 2001: 5–6).

Lib Dem economic policy has been more distinctive in microeconomic contexts; that is to say, when it has urged tax or spending adjustments for a specific political purpose. In 1992, Ashdown proposed to impose an extra penny on income tax, ring-fenced for £2 billion of educational spending, and Lib Dems believed that his focus on the issue over the next few years forced the incoming Blair government to make education a priority in 1997. The party revived this idea in 2017, but now for the NHS. The 2010 manifesto suggested distributing extra funding to schools in which more children were eligible for free school meals (the "pupil premium") and the establishment of a green investment bank to support targeted infrastructure spending. Both schemes were implemented by the Cameron–Clegg coalition government of 2010–15.

From the beginning of Ashdown's leadership, the Lib Dems also increased their focus on environmental policy; he made it one of his five themes in the 1992 election (together with Europe, the economy, education and electoral reform). Lib Dem environmentalism was triggered partly by external factors that also affected other parties: throughout the Western world there was heightened awareness in the 1980s of the impact of industrial emissions, for example on the ozone layer, and a new interest in sustainable development, addressed in the 1987 United Nations Brundtland Report. What the Lib Dems brought to these issues was a tradition of protecting rights of access to a healthy environment, which restrictive landowners and polluting manufacturers might often threaten. This tradition stemmed from the 1860s: Liberal MPs were active in the Commons Preservation Society established in 1865, and in the successive stages of the process by which London's royal parks were fully opened to the people. The 1894 Local Government Act gave democratically elected parish councils the power to maintain public footpaths, to protect public rights of way when threatened and to purchase land for public benefit, leading to a great growth of local recreation grounds. The 1928 *Yellow Book* proposed the preservation of open spaces – the Peak and Lake Districts, Dartmoor and the South Downs – on the principle that public authorities were best placed to balance the competing public goods of economic growth and environmental preservation. This was essentially a policy of extending town planning to the countryside.

So environmentalism was a natural consequence of Liberal refusal to be beholden to the private profit dictates of producer interests. In addition, elements in the party had been proposing more attention to environmental protection throughout the 1970s, especially after the emergence in 1975 of the Ecology Party (the predecessor of the Green Party), which took 1.5 per cent of the vote in the 53 constituencies in which it fielded candidates at the 1979 election. There were tentative discussions about pacts, and in 1979, the Liberal Assembly passed a motion recognizing the impracticability of sustained economic growth. The emergence of Thatcherism, and the influx of SDP members, then helped to marginalize this radical ecological element. The party leadership was well aware of the need to avoid the appearance of opposing economic growth. However, environment-minded Liberals dominated internal party policy-making after 1988, especially with the backing of Ashdown. Moreover, the European elections of 1989, in which the Green Party with 14 per cent took more votes than the Lib Dems, rang alarm bells throughout the party. Ashdown steered it to adopt the principle of "sustainable growth". In 1996 the party endorsed the phased introduction of a carbon tax, while it emphasized environmentalism in all its election manifestoes.

The challenges of party realignment

Liberal and Liberal Democrat history has been punctuated by a series of small-scale electoral breakthroughs. Several have been substantial enough to appear to foreshadow a proper assault on the rigidities of the two-party system. Yet none has had the hoped-for transformative impact.

Russell, Gladstone and Asquith all believed that good government required firm, reliable majorities in the House of Commons, which

Liberal ministries should use to pass a steady stream of high-profile legislation. Yet in the 1920s, the Liberal Party switched tack and urged the need for electoral change, and specifically PR, to prevent over-mighty executive government. In 1922, the Asquithian Liberals tacked PR onto their manifesto for the first time, as a coda to a long complaint about the unprincipled and illiberal Lloyd George coalition government, which they said had substituted "autocratic for Parliamentary Government" because of its large cross-party majority.

Once the Conservative–Labour duopoly was established, the Liberal argument for PR focused on the inability of either party to govern well. Liberals complained that both were monolithic blocs favouring big economic interests or classes. The more practical reason for Liberal focus on PR, of course, is that in a first-past-the-post system their number of parliamentary seats has never matched their percentage share of the vote (although it nearly did in 2024). In ten general elections between 1974 and 2010, the Liberal Party and its successor only once took less than 15 per cent of the vote at an election. But it never won more than 25 seats (out of well over 600), until the Conservative collapse of 1997 allowed it between 46 and 62 during the next 13 years, mainly in the south and southwest.

Unsurprisingly, the two main parties have not supported the case for PR at Westminster. If they can secure a majority in the House of Commons, the party whips can usually enforce the passage of most of their policies. PR is the Liberals' best chance of escaping from permanent third-party status, but it would require them to be in a political position strong enough to impose it on their rivals.

Their alternative hope is a break-up of the existing party system. Liberals have usually envisaged this happening through a realignment of the left, a reversal of the Labour triumph of the 1920s. However, the structural obstacles to this have been formidable.

Grimond encouraged talk of a realignment of the left after the 1959 election, when Labour appeared doomed to electoral defeat and split over revisionism. Sometimes he talked about cooperating with Labour, but sometimes about replacing it (Jones 2011: 19–21). His shift of tone, compared to the previous era of implicit Liberal–Conservative cooperation, made him look more left wing than he actually was. His aim was not to celebrate Labour values but to exploit Labour weakness after the loss of a third successive election. Positioning the Liberals as contributors to a progressive coalition suggested that Labour was not capable of governing on its own. Ironically, the Liberal revival of the early 1960s then ensured that this talk got nowhere. It was the increase in the Liberal vote at Conservative expense, rather than a shift to Labour, that gave Harold Wilson the narrowest of victories at the 1964 election. Wilson had no intention of giving Grimond any more electoral momentum by inviting him into a coalition. He relied instead on building up Labour's own electoral credibility and gained a much larger majority in 1966.

The formation of the SDP in 1981 initially appeared to offer much better prospects for a realignment of the left. But the increase in the Alliance's percentage vote in 1983 was mirrored by a fall in seats, since most former Labour MPs failed to hold theirs. The SDP signally failed to make inroads into Labour's working-class urban heartlands. Good publicity for the Alliance just gave them a slightly better chance in areas in which the Liberals were already doing well. Successive Labour leaders then slowly steered their party back to the electoral centre ground. Despite the loss of a fourth successive election in 1992, most Labour figures rejected any need for party realignment, especially after the Tories were badly damaged by the "Black Wednesday" economic crisis in September 1992 and then by a series of allegations about sleaze.

In the late 1980s, the Lib Dems positioned themselves equidistantly between the other two parties, reflecting their claim that both were extremist. Paddy Ashdown progressively abandoned this position after 1992 and stepped up his attacks on the Conservative government. Chris Rennard, the party's director of campaigns, targeted disaffected Conservative voters. The Lib Dems gained four by-elections in the 1992–7 parliament, and then more than doubled their representation in 1997 to 46 seats. Anti-Tory tactical voting in their target seats seems to have produced between 10 and 14 of these gains (Butler & Kavanagh 1997: 313).

This tactical voting was mirrored by increasingly visible cooperation between the Labour and Lib Dem leaderships. Tony Blair, elected Labour leader in 1994, saw this as part of his challenge to conventional Labour Party culture. Ashdown and he held regular secret meetings. The most important fruit was a bipartisan Joint Consultative Committee on Constitutional Reform, established in 1996, headed by Robin Cook for Labour and Robert Maclennan for the Lib Dems. It drove the constitutional reform agenda discussed in Chapter 5, but its real purpose in Ashdown's eyes was to push Labour towards endorsing PR (Ashdown 2000: 353–4). The Cook–Maclennan Agreement of March 1997 committed the incoming Labour government to appoint an official commission on the voting system, which was headed by the SDP doyen Roy Jenkins. The Jenkins Commission recommended single-member constituencies elected on the AV system, plus 100 MPs elected on regional lists.

The Cook–Maclennan Agreement implied that Lib–Lab cooperation might be needed after a close result in the forthcoming election. Instead, Blair gained a large majority. For a while, it looked as if he still wanted a merger of liberal-left parties; he talked regretfully of the split in progressive forces in the 1910s. Ashdown certainly believed him. But political gravity ultimately reasserted itself. Most Lib Dems never trusted Blair or the centralizing elements within Labour. More to the point, there was no way of reconciling the Labour Party to the idea. Jenkins's electoral recommendations were ignored, to Ashdown's fury. By the time of Blair's second big election victory of 2001, it looked as if he had realigned the left all on his own.

The other option open to Liberals seeking to break the mould of politics has been an arrangement to prop up the government of another party in exchange for promises of some sort about electoral reform. However, such scenarios are infrequent and options often limited: when the February 1974 and 2010 elections returned hung parliaments, the party's MPs realized that they were unlikely to get much credit for keeping in office a prime minister who had just lost his attempt to secure a mandate during an economic crisis, as Edward Heath and Gordon Brown had both done. The Lib–Lab pact of 1977–8, which kept James Callaghan's minority Labour government in office, did David Steel's Liberals relatively little harm, not least because they did not enter government, and because the pact ended a year before the 1979 election. It boosted their visibility as serious political players, which was Steel's aim, but they failed to persuade the government to introduce PR for the 1979 European elections.

For a long time, Liberals and Lib Dems were so convinced of the defects of a first-past-the-post electoral system that they assumed that they could demand PR as a prerequisite for entering a coalition government. Menzies Campbell, briefly party leader in 2006–7, said that coalition on any other terms was inconceivable (Hickson 2009: 71). But this stance was unrealistic. When the 2010 election produced a hung parliament, Campbell's successor, Nick Clegg, took a different and more pragmatic view when the Conservative Party leader David Cameron offered the Lib Dems a share of power in government (although this also reflected his limited experience of, and interest in, the priorities of long-serving Liberal constituency political activists). The Lib Dems entered a full coalition with Cameron's Conservatives while receiving a promise of a referendum on the introduction of the AV system. Meanwhile, the Lib Dem ministers in the new government were determined to show that cross-party government of the sort that PR would regularize could be conducted maturely and responsibly; something that, after the event, they strongly believed they had done. Among Lib Dem inputs to the coalition were the pupil premium (see page 116), the socially progressive increase in the personal income tax allowance, Vince Cable's interventionist industrial strategy and the defence of the Human Rights Act against Conservative attempts to weaken it (Liberal Democrat History Group 2016).

In the 2011 referendum, however, the AV proposal was rejected by 68 to 32 per cent, with both main parties campaigning against it. It was supported in only 10 of 440 voting areas, including Oxford, Cambridge, Edinburgh and a few London boroughs where many electors were highly educated professionals who were interested in such issues. Although supporters of PR complained that AV was a poor substitute, and that the nature of the debate put their cause at a disadvantage, it demonstrated a lack of popular enthusiasm for adjusting the electoral system.

At any time, a coalition arrangement is a risky strategy for a third party, because any show of support for one main party, as against the other, seems to involve taking sides. In 1924, the Liberals lost 40 per cent of their vote after putting in a Labour government for nine months. In 2015, the Lib Dems lost 60 per cent of their vote for supporting a Conservative government in full coalition for five years. They were squeezed by the return of two-party polarization after the coalition experiment. Right-leaning voters opted for the Conservatives, for fear of a Labour–Scottish National Party (SNP) "coalition of chaos", while some left-leaning ones associated the Lib Dems with harsh Conservative economic policies and particularly the flagship programme of austerity after the financial crisis. Clegg had wanted to drop the Lib Dems' pledge of 2005 to abolish university tuition fees, but the 2010 manifesto retained it. It was very popular with students at the 2010 election, and the party suffered enormously when, in response to the Browne Review of university funding, the coalition instead felt it necessary to increase fees from £3,290 to a maximum of £9,000. It suffered further from George Osborne's 2012 budget, when he cut the top rate of income tax from 50p to 45p. Labour labelled it a "budget for millionaires", the Conservative and Lib Dem vote share fell, and Osborne was booed at the London Olympics that summer. He had previously boasted that the response to austerity was a joint national effort: that we were "all in it together". Tax cuts for the rich, while public services were being cut, gave a disastrously different impression, of favouring the few rather than the many.

The experience of coalition also badly damaged Lib Dem performance at local government level. In retrospect, however, the damage was relatively short term. The party's strongest and most resilient asset remains its electoral base in those local communities where it has forged an identity as the practitioner of a distinctive and successful form of politics.

In the 1960s, the most prominent Liberal local government victories came in the large towns. Wallace Lawler became a city councillor in Birmingham in 1962 and briefly an MP in 1969–70, focusing on homelessness (plus some anti-immigrant rhetoric). The Liberal group led by Cyril Carr and Trevor Jones built up a position on Liverpool City Council from 1962, taking it over in 1973. This brought "Jones the Vote" national fame for his organizational skills, which included the pioneering distribution to each letterbox of regular "Focus" newsletters on local problems. In recognition of these early victories, an Association of Liberal Councillors emerged in 1965 and was officially recognized in 1969.

Encouraged by these developments, a band of Young Liberals, led by Gordon Lishman and Lawrence Freedman, publicized a philosophy of community politics in 1969–70. After the disappointment of the 1970 election result, the chair of the Young Liberals, Tony Greaves, successfully committed the party Assembly to their approach of building a power base in the major cities through community campaigns. This was presented not just as a question of winning votes and council seats but of creating a more participatory and engaged local political culture, based on the self-acting individual who would be energized into "mutual and individual responsibility" through community activity on the principles of liberty and interdependence (Jones 2011: 63). It was fuelled by the same Liberal dislike of monolithic and centralized two-party politics that Grimond had campaigned against. Central government and local authorities both seemed in thrall to powerful sectional interests; at local level this had created postwar housing blight. The idea of community activism as an antidote to bleakly interest-dominated national politics drew strength from history: from the initiatives of the late 1870s undertaken by Joseph Chamberlain in Birmingham and T. H. Green in Oxford. Lishman was clear that the Young Liberals had developed the case for community politics themselves, but that these precedents pointed to the strength and coherence of the Liberal tradition (Jones 2011: 62).

In practice, community politics in most places was based on a remorseless attention to voters' concerns about neighbourhood housing, development and public transport issues, however small-scale, including the state of paving stones, road potholes and council estate gardens. Moreover, it worked best where there were a significant number of local activists who had the leisure, experience and education necessary to devote large amounts of time to local politics; many of these were retired. Over time, this meant a shift away from the large towns, where Labour remains generally very strong, to suburbs and smaller communities. Liberals had lost control of Liverpool council by 1983 (although the Lib Dems regained it from 1998 to 2010, when Labour was in power nationally). An early example of the party's ability to appeal to the suburban vote was the parliamentary by-election victory of the local councillor Graham Tope in Sutton and Cheam in 1972. His seat was not held for long, but much of southwest London later became a Lib Dem stronghold.

The Liberal revival of the early 1970s gave the party 1,474 councillors in 1974, falling to 923 in 1978. In the 1980s, effective local campaigning dovetailed neatly with the party's national self-projection as an unthreatening, sensible middle-ground force: its number of council seats rose from 1,850 in 1982 to 2,971 in 1986 (524 of which were the SDP's) and 3,640 in 1987. During the anti-Conservative reaction of the 1990s, it grew further, reaching a peak of 5,078 in 1996, against the Conservative Party's 4,276; the Lib Dems then controlled over 50 councils (Rallings & Thrasher 2007: 226). During Blair's honeymoon period, the Lib Dems lost 20 councils, but after 2001 their number of councillors revived to a lower peak of 4,743 in 2005. The turbulent politics of the 2010s led to major losses, and as of 2024 they still had only 3,100 councillors, but these were better concentrated, so that the Lib Dems were the lead party in government in nearly 70 councils, mostly in the south and west.

When their number of MPs more than doubled in 1997, gains included a swathe of English seats in generally affluent places where the party already controlled the council, such as Cheltenham, Colchester, Eastleigh, Harrogate and Hereford. As Ashdown remarked in 2001, Lib Dem MPs' experience in running local councils helped immeasurably to professionalize the party's image in comparison with the idiosyncratic and free-wheeling individuals who had dominated it in the 1970s (Ashdown 2001: 6–7). In the 2020s, Lib Dem operations at council level continue to showcase the benefits of local decision-making and citizen participation. This self-projection has given them a core electoral support, illustrating the relevance of their model of democratic engagement even at a time of profound disillusionment with the political process.

The 2020s

In the 2023 local elections, the Lib Dems won control of a dozen councils, mostly in suburban and commuter England. Then, at the 2024 general election, they targeted Conservative seats in the south and west and won almost all of them. This reflected a high degree of antipathy to the 2019–24 Conservative government among affluent and professional-class voters, a continuing hostility to Brexit in particular and a lack of concern about the economic consequences of letting Labour into office. The party also benefited from anti-Tory tactical voting in its target seats, and therefore from the broader Labour and media attack on the government. This wider anti-Tory mood had two general and two specific causes. The general ones were the state of public services after many years of austerity and the impact on the economy and living standards caused by a mixture of Brexit, Covid-19 and the Ukraine war. Criticism was intensified by two episodes that speak to key themes of this book.

Boris Johnson's popularity as prime minister was destroyed because of the perception that he and his friends had not suffered along with the rest of the nation during the 2020–21 Covid pandemic, and that indeed many Tories had benefited from it. Stories about parties in 10 Downing Street suggested that Johnson and his aides had not followed the government's own tough restrictions on personal liberty that forced millions to make repeated sacrifices of companionship, earnings and freedom during lockdown. The media luxuriated in details about the refurbishment of the prime minister's flat and the eye-wateringly expensive wallpaper apparently required by his wife. The shock of the pandemic exposed the government to wider criticism of "sleaze" and incompetence over the award of Covid-related contracts to companies with connections to the Conservative Party. Johnson tried to prevent the suspension of one Conservative MP, Owen Paterson, when the Commons Select Committee on Standards criticized him for lobbying government agencies on behalf of a diagnostics firm and a sausage manufacturer that paid him for lobbying services. This was a return to the theme of "old corruption" that had driven popular radicalism before the first Reform Act.

Likewise, Liz Truss's brief premiership of 2022 made it easy for opponents to argue that Tories benefited the wealthy, at the expense of the public and of good government. She and her chancellor announced £45 billion of tax cuts by 2026, reducing the basic rate and abolishing the 45 per cent rate for those earning over £150,000 per year. They claimed this package would stimulate the economy so rapidly that it could be financed merely with extra short-term borrowing, without spending cuts. The financial markets reacted very badly to the idea of unfunded tax cuts. Mortgage rates jumped dramatically to over 6 per cent, and lenders withdrew over 40 per cent of their products. A run on bonds threatened pension fund solvency. The proposed abolition of the 45 per cent tax rate made the government look out of touch and uninterested in class fairness. Between August and October 2022, the percentage of the public supporting the Conservative Party in opinion polls fell from 33 to 22 per cent, and the number approving of government performance fell from 19 to 8 per cent. The Truss affair showed how vulnerable Tories remain if they lose their reputation for economic competence, and especially if voters perceive that they are a vested interest party keen to support a privileged class.

In 2024, the Lib Dems took 72 seats, more than at any election since 1923, on 12 per cent of the vote. Many of their seat majorities were large: they took over 50 per cent of the vote in 18 constituencies and 45 per cent or more in another 17. In these core seats, they boast a very professional organization. They have often mobilized local opinion for purposeful campaigns: fighting river pollution, demanding local hospitals. Many of their MPs have backgrounds in local business or public sector organizations. But their fate will still depend largely on the behaviour of their opponents. Labour government policy on taxation will help to determine whether voters in these seats feel that they need to revert to voting Conservative. The Conservative Party may have to choose between wooing back voters lost to the Lib Dems or the very different social groups that it lost to the Reform Party.

The party's 2024 campaign focused on practical issues such as sewage emissions, as well as a series of eye-catching stunts by leader Ed Davey designed to bring the party to voters' attention, including bungee-jumping and falling off a paddleboard on Lake Windermere. There was nothing here to upset affluent and disillusioned Conservatives in target seats. After the election, some Lib Dem activists criticized this approach for the loss of idealistic young people to the Greens, and the failure to make an impact in most midland and northern constituencies (Whiting 2024). Over 80 per cent of their candidates won less than 15 per cent of the vote.

However, this chapter has downplayed the extent to which the party's fortunes have been affected by its stance on economic policy. Perceptions of the party's position on the political spectrum have depended much less on its policy positions than on whether it has been trapped into appearing dependent on one of the main two parties. The party has from time to time made radical moves in specific policy areas, without incurring much criticism that its whole approach is dangerously socialistic. The Lib Dems cannot replace the Conservative Party on the right, but they may be aiming to keep it there: to limit its revival, thus encouraging the perception that it is a mere sectional force, not the natural party of government that it claims to be. This would entrench the sense that multiparty politics is here to stay, which would in turn encourage talk about PR.

Liberals and Lib Dems' economic policies have rarely made headlines. Whenever they have been distinctive, it is because of their political rather than their economic ramifications: because they have projected a sense of purposeful dynamism, attacked specific vested interests or tried to promote party realignment. The Lib Dems' fundamental scepticism about state bureaucracy transcends the conventional "left–right" economic debate. It derives instead from their greater concern, which remains, as always, the overcentralization of power.

5

Modern Liberalism and power: devolution, liberties and Europe

Liberal concern with the distribution of power has given the party a distinctive interest in several constitutional issues in addition to PR. The most important have been civil liberties, devolution to localities, and British relations with Europe and the wider world.

For decades, Liberal MPs have argued that British politics is "broken", because the centralized United Kingdom state has excessive control and the two parties that compete for office have a vested interest in maintaining it. At the 1950 general election, Jo Grimond wrote that "it was not strong government we needed, but less government, better government and government nearer home" (Sell 1997–8: 7). In 1988, Alan Beith noted that the Liberals' one big idea was "that the relationship between the individual and institutional power must be transformed" (Jones 2011: 144). Liberals have suggested that politics needs a reset if it is to respond effectively to the grievances of citizens and provide good government respectful of their liberties. The parallels with the nineteenth-century Reform Acts are obvious.

For most of the twentieth century, Liberal ambitions for constitutional reform focused on PR and devolution, but in successive election manifestoes between 1979 and 1987 they widened into something more systematic. This culminated in the Great Reform Charter unveiled in 1987 in an explicit nod to the nineteenth-century Reform tradition. Its ten pledges included PR for the British and European parliaments, a Freedom of Information Bill, the incorporation of the European Convention on Human Rights into a British Bill of Rights, the outlawing of all discrimination on grounds of race, sex, creed, class, disability or sexual orientation, the introduction of fixed-term parliaments, the creation of a Scottish Assembly, Welsh Senedd and English regional bodies, and procedural reform to the Commons and Lords.

These proposals then made the Lib Dems important players in the wider discussions about the need to update constitutional rights, which resulted from the electoral dominance of Margaret Thatcher on less than 43 per cent of the vote and her zealous pursuit of reforms that were clearly unpopular in Scotland, Wales and the north of Britain. Her third victory in 1987 led to the emergence of Charter 88 and of the Scottish Claim of Right, both pursuing this agenda. These developments in turn influenced a move in the Labour Party, after its fourth successive electoral defeat, to consider constitutional reform more sympathetically. When Tony Blair became leader, he declared in favour of Scottish and Welsh devolution, Freedom of Information, a Bill of Rights and other reforms at the 1994 Labour Party Conference.

For the Labour Party, one benefit of adopting this agenda was in case it needed allies after the next election. In 1995–6, Labour and the Lib Dems inched towards formal talks, with the aim of agreeing on a detailed package of constitutional reforms. As both parties had already accepted all the key principles, the object was clearly to work out the terms of a joint programme if cooperation in government became necessary. The two parties established a Joint Consultative Committee on Constitutional Reform under co-chairs Robin Cook and Robert Maclennan. In March 1997, the Cook–Maclennan Agreement established the ground-rules for all the constitutional reforms subsequently enacted by the first Blair government. The bulk of the 1987 Great Reform Charter was addressed. Moreover, between 1997 and 2001 five Lib Dem MPs sat on a government committee that scrutinized the government's bills before they were published. But Labour and the Lib Dems later fell out, at first over Blair's unwillingness to implement the recommendations of the Jenkins Commission on electoral reform and later over civil liberties and the Iraq War.

The story of this Lib Dem constitutional reform package therefore has a double significance: in itself, and in the part that it played in one particular chapter in the story of attempted party realignment in Britain. Likewise, the Europe issue had been integral to the previous attempt at a realignment of the left in the late 1970s and early 1980s. Entry into the EEC in 1973 was a major episode in postwar British history, but the cooperation of pro-Europeans in the cause also pointed the way towards the creation of the SDP–Liberal Alliance. The Liberal Party had been the first major party to advocate joining the EEC, in 1959, and was the most comfortable in arguing that sharing national sovereignty would help to tackle pressing international issues. In the aftermath of Brexit, this position gave the Lib Dems their most distinctive position in the mid-2020s. The two-party system looks unprecedentedly vulnerable to attack from a resurgent third party, but that party might be either a pro-European one (the Lib Dems) or a populist anti-European one (Nigel Farage's Reform Party). European policy continues to be bound up with the future shape of the political system itself.

Devolution

The Liberal Party necessarily favoured a significant degree of Scottish self-government. Liberalism had become the dominant force in Scottish politics immediately after the 1832 Reform Act. The Scottish Liberal Party was a coalition of Whig landlords (shut out of power before 1832 by the Tory network that had run Scottish politics), ambitious merchants and university-educated lawyers in the big towns, and Free Churchmen who had no taste for English Tory Anglicanism. In the 1880s, it was rejuvenated also by the Highland crofters' struggles for security of tenure against eviction, which many local Free Church ministers joined (MacColl 2006). Historically, Scottish civil society was soaked in radical individualism and Presbyterian communitarianism, and outside the central urban belt this continued to be the case until the 1960s at least. Except at the wartime election of 1900, Liberals took a clear majority of Scottish seats at every election until the First World War.

Although the English and Scottish Crowns were united in 1603, Scotland remained a separate country. The new parliament of Great Britain established by the Act of Union in 1707 had very limited legislative ambitions. Scotland retained its own legal system, with a greater continental and Roman law component than England's, and a different common law tradition. Scotland had a separate education system and a different, Presbyterian, Established Church. When parliament reformed its representation in 1832 and 1867, Scotland's seats were restructured on different principles by separate Reform Acts. Meanwhile, local elites had the powers they needed to govern their own towns, as in England.

Once government started to increase its legislative ambitions, it did not take long before, in 1894, Liberal MPs secured the establishment of a Scottish Grand Committee of MPs, to consider draft bills relating to the country. The following year, the Conservatives abolished it – Arthur Balfour argued that MPs should not concern themselves particularly with legislation for a specific territory – but it was reconstituted by the Campbell-Bannerman government in 1907, so that Scottish bills could be discussed by Scottish MPs on Scottish principles (Mitchell 2014: 74–7). A secretary for Scotland was established in 1885. Once the Liberal Party took up Irish Home Rule in 1886, many Scotsmen asked for the same. The aim was not separation: most of them hoped to relieve parliamentary congestion and find time for the consideration of local issues. "Home Rule all round" the four countries of the United Kingdom was also connected with the idea of imperial federation, which was a particular enthusiasm of Lord Rosebery, Scotland's leading Liberal (Kidd 2008: 276–9). In 1913, Asquith's government promised a Scottish Home Rule Bill.

After the First World War, Liberal representation in Scotland fell dramatically, but this was less of a change in political culture than it might appear. Most MPs who supported Scottish "Conservatism" came from Liberal traditions: from Scottish Liberal Unionism, strengthened after 1931 by a significant number of Liberal Nationals. Scottish Liberal Unionism was founded on the economic and cultural ties between Ulster and the intensely Protestant west of Scotland. When Scottish Conservatives merged formally with the Liberal Unionists in 1912, they called themselves the Scottish Unionist Party, not Conservatives. Unionism stood for resistance to control from the metropolitan state; this remained a popular agenda after 1945, as the economic powers of the London government grew. Only in the late 1950s – once Conservative governments in London became more confident and more interventionist – did rural Scottish voters come to feel that the Unionists might not be the best defenders of a Scottish anti-metropolitan identity. Scottish Liberalism and Nationalism both revived as a result (Petrie 2022: 27–32, 42–4, 58–61).

In 1955, Grimond was Scotland's sole bona fide Liberal MP, but the party's re-emergence in the 1960s and 1970s had its deepest roots in rural Scotland. Four of the party's six leaders between 1956 and 2007 were Scots. In 1964, the party gained three seats in the Highlands, having campaigned for regional regeneration: successfully, as their pressure led to the establishment of the Highlands and Islands Development Board in 1965 (Finnie 2011: 29). David Steel won in the Borders in 1965. Grimond got the party committed to the idea of a Scottish parliament. Meanwhile the SNP emerged powerfully, winning two important by-election victories in 1967 and 1973 and 11 seats in October 1974. These victories led Harold Wilson's Labour government to establish a Royal Commission in 1969, which produced the Kilbrandon report recommending devolution for Scotland and Wales in 1973. However, the idea of devolution initially posed great problems for a Labour Party that believed in centralizing power in order to socialize the economy. The 1974–9 Labour government fell after its mishandling of the issue.

A consensus emerged on devolution during the 1980s, in response to the imposition of Thatcherism from Westminster, specifically its attack on trade unions and its introduction of a regressive poll tax. After Thatcher's third election victory in 1987, Labour, Liberal, trade union and community leaders began a movement for a Scottish Assembly. In March 1989, their Claim of Right, declaring "the sovereign right of the Scottish people to determine the form of Government best suited to their needs", was signed by most MPs, MEPs and council leaders. For the next six years, a Scottish Constitutional Convention debated the principles of devolved government. It quickly rejected independence, so the SNP withdrew from it. Church and trade union leaders were actively involved, but the main impetus behind it was cross-party collaboration between the leading Scottish Labour politicians and Lib Dems Russell Johnston, David Steel, Robert Maclennan and Jim Wallace.

This extensive civic collaboration laid down the principles of the Scottish devolution settlement that the Blair government enacted in 1998–9. Both parties hoped that Lab–Lib cooperation would dominate politics in a devolved Scotland. The settlement included an element of PR for the Scottish Parliament: in addition to 73 MSPs elected on a first-past-the-post basis, party popularity in each region would determine the allocation of 56 other seats. This limited degree of PR was acceptable to the Scottish Labour Party, partly because of the need for compromise with the Lib Dems, partly from genuine optimism about the possibilities of a new approach to politics, but partly also from anxiety about the rise of the SNP, which took over 21 per cent of the vote in 1992.

A Lab–Lib government was established after the first elections in 1999 and lasted until 2007. It saw itself as forming a constructive partnership with the Blair regime in London. The most significant Lib Dem contribution came from the Scottish party's leader, Jim Wallace, who became deputy first minister and minister of justice. He secured a raft of measures with a focus on civil liberties issues, among them significantly stronger freedom of information legislation than in England (including a straightforward right of access to information and fewer grounds for exemption), and land reform that gave walkers the right to roam and enabled community buyouts of land put up for sale. In addition, civil marriages were allowed outside a registry office, and criminal justice reforms gave more power to victims, while PR (the single transferable vote) was introduced for Scottish local elections (Lindsay 2014).

Though the Scottish executive had extensive responsibilities, almost all of them had previously been delegated to Scottish-based civil servants. It was given modest tax-raising powers, but 90 per cent of its revenue came from London, and Gordon Brown was determined to maintain Treasury control over it. This arrangement was ripe for exploitation by the SNP, and after 2007 it dominated Scottish politics by appealing to those who wanted devolved government to be more ambitious, culturally distinctive and assertive against London. SNP pressure forced David Cameron's coalition government to cede a referendum on the union in 2014. The unionist parties issued a joint "Vow" to expand the range of devolved powers if it was defeated. As a result, the Scottish Parliament and government were made permanent, and Westminster agreed not to legislate on Scottish matters without the Parliament's support. The Act also increased the Scottish government's tax-varying powers. Scotland could now raise 40 per cent of its revenue.

A genuine multiparty politics emerged in Scotland, but the Lib Dems lost out as a result. Other options were always available for Scottish voters dissatisfied with government in London or Edinburgh. They took four Scottish seats in the 2019 general election and six in 2024, with 9.5 per cent and 9.7 per cent of the vote, an increase on their electoral performance in Scotland during the 2010 coalition but a long way short of the 15–16 per cent share that they had gained in the 2003 and 2007 Scottish elections, when they were still seen as significant players in government.

The question of devolution for Wales always followed in the Scottish slipstream, and a referendum in 1979 had rejected the idea of a separate assembly by a margin of four to one. Wales lacked Scotland's rich pre-Union constitutional history. There was no separate Crown, parliament or legal system. With industrialization, the centre of demographic and political gravity shifted to the urban south, where Labour values took deep root. The Labour Party won half the Welsh seats for the first time as early as 1922 and has dominated Principality politics ever since. The Blair government could not avoid legislating on the subject, and introduced a devolved Welsh Assembly with modest powers in 1999, after a new referendum narrowly approved the idea. The logic of the scheme, endorsed by the Cook–Maclennan Agreement, was to provide democratic control over the administrative functions that had been devolved to the Welsh Office and to non-elected quangos.

As it happened, the initial elections gave the Lib Dems enough seats to make a Lab–Lib coalition possible, but this was much less harmonious than the Scottish example owing to culture clashes, and both sides were reluctant to repeat the experiment (Deacon 2014). Welsh Liberalism had been strong in the nineteenth century, fuelled by resentment of the Anglo-Welsh gentry and by Nonconformist hostility to the (gentry-influenced) Established Church. But this waned once the landlords lost their power and the Church was disestablished (by the Lloyd George coalition in 1920), and especially once Lloyd George's small family party of MPs broke up. Such influence as Liberalism retained from the 1950s was dependent on individuals, who tended to be barristers, since they could fund themselves and spoke well, but their need to earn money made them part-time MPs, the classic case being Roderic Bowen, MP for Ceredigion 1945–66. Welsh nationalism emerged in rural Welsh-speaking areas in the 1960s and 1970s, captured most of the Liberals' old seats and pushed the Liberals into fourth place in Principality politics (Deacon 2005–6). By the 2020s, Lib Dem numbers both at Westminster and at the Senedd were reduced to one, reflecting the party's weakness outside the border area of Brecon and Radnor. At the 2024 general election, it won 6.5 per cent of the vote throughout the Principality.

New Labour and civil liberties

The cross-party talks that created the Scottish devolution scheme provided the precedent for the Labour–Lib Dem discussions of 1996–7 on a wider constitutional reform package. These discussions, by the Joint Consultative Committee on Constitutional Reform, had a varied impact after 1997, depending on the specific issues involved. Blair's Labour government was naturally keenest on those elements that removed impediments to its own power, as for example with House of Lords reform and the creation of an elected London mayoralty. Progress also depended on the enthusiasms of individual cabinet ministers: John Prescott was the keenest on English devolution, but his plans were defeated in a local referendum in the north-east. The Cook–Maclennan Agreement specified the appointment of a Commission on an alternative voting system for Westminster elections and the holding of a referendum on its recommendation, but the Blair government failed to honour the second pledge, damaging cross-party relations badly. So the main practical impact of the agreement was seen in two areas of legislation: civil liberties and human rights. Yet in the end the parties fell out over civil liberties as well.

Freedom of information was a long-standing Liberal theme: Grimond had complained about departmental secrecy in the 1950s and 1960s. The Freedom of Information Act 2000 created a statutory right of access to information held by most public authorities, although the promises of the government's initial White Paper on the subject had already been watered down. In retrospect, Blair described himself as a "naïve, foolish, irresponsible nincompoop" for agreeing to the 2000 Act: "I quake at the imbecility of it". He claimed it was a weapon not for "the people" but for hostile journalists (Blair 2010: 516–17). After the September 2001 terrorist attacks in the United States, the government became unhappier with the Act's implications, invoking security needs and the terror threat. Yet it survived unamended. During the Cameron coalition government, in 2012–13, a Justice Select Committee investigation chaired by Alan Beith concluded that the Act had enhanced democracy and changed the culture of central government. It was confident that the Act's provisions (which included the option of a ministerial veto) adequately protected confidentiality in the handling of sensitive matters.

As chancellor and aspirant prime minister, Gordon Brown made speeches in the mid-2000s advertising his libertarianism. He talked of a "golden thread running through British history . . . of the individual standing firm against tyranny and then – an even more generous, expansive view of liberty – the idea of government accountable to the people" (Brown 2006). Sceptics interpreted these interventions as cover to pursue an overtly illiberal line on two specific issues: the introduction of identity cards and the detention of suspected terrorists. In 2003, Home Secretary David Blunkett announced that, in pursuit of the war on terror, the government intended to introduce a "British national identity card" linked to a national identity database, the National Identity Register. A bill to this effect encountered strong opposition when it was introduced, before the 2005 general election and again after it. There was particular concern about the 50 categories of information that the government wanted to hold on individuals on its database, as well as about the expense. The Act of 2006 passed into law only after the House of Lords made the scheme voluntary for British citizens. The Act, and the National Identity Register, was abolished by the Cameron coalition government in 2011. Liberals had consistently opposed the idea of identity cards. In 1950–51, the Liberal councillor and parliamentary candidate Harry Willcock led the campaign against the cards that had been introduced by emergency legislation on the outbreak of war in 1939, and that the postwar Labour government continued, ostensibly to facilitate the administration of food rationing. The police could prosecute people for failing to produce the card, as happened to Willcock when he was stopped for speeding in Finchley. Declaring "I am a Liberal, and I am against this sort of thing", he appealed against his conviction in the High Court, stirring up a national debate about abolition. He launched a Freedom Defence Committee by destroying his own card in front of photographers on the steps of the National Liberal Club. In February 1952, the requirement to carry the cards was lifted (Egan 1997–8).

After the attack on the Twin Towers in September 2001, followed by the London bombings of July 2005, Blair's government wanted more powers against terrorism. The Anti-Terrorism Crime and Security Act passed in December 2001 allowed the home secretary to order the indefinite detention of foreign terrorist suspects. In December 2004, the Law Lords declared this incompatible with the human rights legislation, discussed in the next section, that the government had itself introduced in 1998. In response, the government passed an Act allowing the home secretary to impose control orders on individuals suspected of involvement in terrorism; these were disallowed by a judge on the same grounds. After the July 2005 bombings, the government proposed to allow those suspected of terrorism offences to be detained without charge for 90 days, virtually abolishing habeas corpus. In November this was defeated in the Commons – the first defeat for the Blair government on a whipped vote – owing to 49 rebel Labour MPs joining the opposition parties including the 62 Lib Dem MPs. The 2006 Terrorism Act extended the allowable detention period from 14 to 28 days, but the coalition government rescinded this extension in 2011.

Behind these issues lay the American and British governments' response to the 2001 attacks itself. Tony Blair's decision to give British support to the Bush administration's declaration of war on Iraq in 2003 was the most momentous of his premiership. The Lib Dems unanimously opposed the war, the only one of the three major parties to do so. They objected to the failure to uphold the processes of international law, which were designed to broker a peaceful outcome, and to the failure to justify the invasion, given the lack of evidence of Iraqi weapons of mass destruction. They criticized the government's attempts to manipulate public opinion by selective release of information, and the refusal to follow the majority public opposition to the war. Party leader Charles Kennedy painted the government's policy as illegal, short-sighted and authoritarian: the culmination of its characteristic greed for excessive constitutional power and disregard for rational public debate (Kennedy 2003). Their stance over Iraq benefited them in opinion polls – they scored over 30 per cent in the 2003 local elections – and boosted their popularity briefly among Muslim voters, leading to some eye-catching by-election victories in places that had not been Liberal targets, such as Brent East in 2003 and Leicester South in 2004 (where the victorious MP was Parmjit Singh Gill, one of very few ethnic minority Lib Dem MPs ever elected).

Human rights and the Liberal tradition

After the Second World War, the politicians and lawyers of western Europe were anxious to entrench constitutional checks against the risk of a return to totalitarian government, whether Nazi or Communist. Parliamentary majorities did not seem to offer a robust enough check in themselves. The idea of a European Convention of Human Rights came out of the desire to secure democracy and the rule of law on the continent, and Britain was the first country to ratify it in 1951. British governments were slow to think that British citizens, secure in the protection of parliament and the common law, needed individual protection through such devices. But it was natural that human rights advocates would come to urge the incorporation of the Convention in British law, since Britain, unlike most other European countries, lacked a modern bill of rights. International campaigns for women's rights and against racial discrimination also highlighted the issue. Liberal parliamentarians Alan Beith and Donald Wade introduced bills for incorporation from 1975, and a bill of rights was included in the Liberal Party's 1979 manifesto. The Labour Party moved towards the same idea in 1993–4 and the Cook–Maclennan Agreement endorsed the proposal.

The 1998 Human Rights Act incorporated into British law a series of human rights taken from the European Convention of Human Rights, so that citizens no longer needed to go to Strasbourg to secure them. Home Secretary Jack Straw followed the Cook–Maclennan Agreement in presenting the legislation as bringing home rights originally developed by Britain. By 2003 the courts had pronounced that current law was rights-incompatible in ten areas. Parliament was not obliged to change the law as a result, but it did so in all cases.

Moreover, the Act put rights-compatibility at the centre of the law-making process. This was a particular concern of the Labour Lord Chancellor, Derry Irvine, a lawyer who had never been an MP. The Act stipulated that governments must demonstrate that future legislative proposals were compatible with these rights. All official consideration of potential new bills now takes place in the consciousness that the courts may be asked to take issue with any aspect that might infringe rights.

As the history of anti-terrorist legislation indicates, the discussion and fate of bills is now heavily shaped by the provisions of the

1998 Act, and even more by the Brown government's Equality Act of 2010. That Act prohibited discrimination, harassment or victimization on grounds of several protected characteristics, including age, disability, gender reassignment, pregnancy, race, belief, sex and sexual orientation. As a result, rights of all sorts have much stronger legal protection. Rights-based reforms generally enjoy a following wind. The Cameron–Clegg coalition government legalized marriages for same sex couples in 2013, owing mainly to work by the Lib Dem minister Lynne Featherstone, with Nick Clegg's support. This strong body of law, together with the establishment of the Supreme Court in 2009, has given the courts a more prominent role in upholding human rights. This has clarified but also narrowed the scope for political debate. Concerns have been raised about democratic scrutiny of the process, a theme that the Cook–Maclennan Agreement had tried to address.

Specific discussions of human rights issues can still create political tensions, from which Liberals have not been immune. There has been a long tradition in British politics that private and sexual morality are matters of individual conscience, on which MPs should vote freely rather than be whipped to support a party line. This applies particularly to tricky ethical issues such as abortion, assisted dying and rights of gender reclassification and surgery. Some MPs will have strong personal principles on such matters; others will feel obliged to respect strongly held public convictions. From a prudential point of view, parties realize that they would probably offend more voters than they attract if they were to enforce a decided line on such nuanced issues. Moreover, not all debates on such issues have been framed primarily in terms of personal freedom of choice. In the postwar era, the single most important contribution of a Liberal MP on ethical issues was the Act to decriminalize abortion introduced by David Steel in 1967 as a private member's bill. The Act was concerned with ethical dilemmas, not with feminist rights. Steel – a practising Christian and the son of a Church of Scotland minister – shaped the bill after consultation with religious leaders and medical practitioners who were immensely disturbed by the number of pregnant women who were forced to resort to unlicensed and unskilled practitioners, sometimes with tragic effects. Their aim was to minimize preventable suffering by striking a better ethical balance between the obvious threat to the health and well-being of the mother and the rights of the foetus (Steel 1989: 50–55). In later years, one of the greatest opponents of the Act was another Liberal parliamentarian, the Liverpool Catholic David Alton.

Values change over time. No one would expect Victorian Liberals to prioritize gay rights, given the degree of opprobrium of homosexuality throughout the nineteenth century. It is sometimes said that John Stuart Mill's *On Liberty* should be a Liberal's bible in all such matters, on account of its defence of the principle of individual freedom. If Mill had confined himself to issues of civil liberty against government power, that would be an easy case to support. But Mill's primary concern was that "individuals are lost in the crowd": that freedom of thought was jeopardized by social pressure from unreflective mass opinion and the "collective mediocrity" that it represented. This, he thought, meant that the "tyranny of the majority" would prevent intellectual advances, imperilling civilisation. He disliked the prevailing lowbrow materialism of the commercial middle class and the potential sectionalism and ignorance of a working-class electorate. He felt that both classes needed a much better education, which should be compulsory. As a free thinker, he felt that the most damaging influence of all was unreflective religious orthodoxy; in itself, and for its deadening impact in many policy areas, including education and the social position of women.

On Liberty was not intended as a political party bible but as a contribution to general educated discourse. It was also intended to be provocative: Mill knew that most Victorians would not agree with his underlying assumptions. Most educated Victorians did not see orthodox religion as a restrictive cultural force. On the contrary, many of them viewed the issue of liberty through a religious lens. Individual responsibility was responsibility and accountability before God. Victorian admiration for individual energies and the individual conscience was founded on the assumption that humans were made in God's image and that setting them free – with guidance from social leaders – would create a more perfect society. Victorians assumed that lawmakers had a Christian responsibility to promote morality and character, as Chapter 2 discussed. Influential British judges continued to assume that they had a moral function, at least until the 1960s (Griffin forthcoming). Britain is now such a secular country that many are surprised to discover surviving remnants of the religious conscience in operation, such as when Tim Farron, the evangelical who led the Lib Dems from 2015 to 2017, voted to uphold the rights of registrars and others not to participate in gay marriage ceremonies if these infringed their personal beliefs (Williams 2017).

Liberalism and European institutions

Liberal internationalism has very deep roots, long predating the development of a powerful European Union (EU). Throughout its time as a great power after 1815, Britain's main strategic interest was the pursuit of international peace, leaving space for its global trade to develop. Some Liberal politicians, such as Richard Cobden and his followers, wanted to reduce diplomacy, which they saw as an expensive and dangerous game of aristocrats, and instead to rely on commerce to show the peoples of the world the benefits of avoiding war. But most of them assumed that the route to peace lay through hard-headed politics: through regular discussions with other European powers, in order to prevent military strongmen from dominating the continent. Chapter 2 discussed British ideas about the European balance of power, including opposition to the bullying of small nations by the autocratic powers of central and eastern Europe. In the 1930s, most Liberal MPs strongly opposed the Munich agreement and Neville Chamberlain's appeasement of Hitler on the same ground. By 1939, the party's then leader, Sir Archibald Sinclair, was openly cooperating with Churchill for a stronger policy (Hunter 2004).

The First and Second World Wars dealt savage blows to Britain's standing in the world. But this underlined that Britain's interest was in the return of peace, prosperity, freer trade and some sort of continental balance of power. Lloyd George has been criticized for supporting tough reparations during the peace negotiations at Versailles, but this reflected intensely strong pressure both from the French and from Conservatives in his government. British diplomacy in the 1920s aimed to reinstate Germany as a prosperous trading partner. At the Bretton Woods Conference of 1944, Keynes made proposals for global tariff liberalization that issued in the General Agreement on Tariffs and Trade, later the World Trade Organization. After 1945, Britain was active in the Marshall Aid programme, and was intimately involved in the organizations set up to re-establish European stability: NATO and the Western Union, as well as the Council of Europe, founded by the

Treaty of London in 1949. Liberals supported membership of NATO because they generally trusted the values of the United States and saw themselves as a junior partner in a liberal project to maintain international economic stability, international peace and liberal capitalism against communism. For the same reason, Liberal leader Clement Davies applauded the idea of a European Coal and Steel Community in 1950 (Sloman 2015: 171).

Jo Grimond became party leader at the time of the Suez crisis of 1956. It supplied him with his main message: that Britain had a duty to reassess its global position rationally and morally, in the light of the Cold War and the end of empire. He positioned the Liberals against imperial nostalgia and the military repression of the Kenyan colonial independence movement. He argued that Western cooperation in NATO would check the threat of nuclear war with Communist Russia, while releasing Britain from the obligation to have its own supposedly independent nuclear deterrent. For the West to pool nuclear resources in a combined deterrent force was the best route to peace and prosperity: to "exchange goods, not H-bombs", as the party's 1959 manifesto put it.

The 1957 Treaty of Rome bound France, Germany, Italy and the three Benelux countries into the EEC. The EEC originally set high external tariffs, to nurture European manufacturing and agriculture, and this posed problems for free trade Liberals. Grimond began by supporting the Conservative government's alternative policy, of building up a European free trade area, but by 1959 he had decided that the EEC offered the best route to European cooperation, even if it did not reduce external tariffs (which it did). The Liberals were the first party to support EEC membership, in 1959, adopting the idea formally in 1960. This involved facing down opposition from Smedleyite free traders (Baines 2004). For Grimond, and for pro-EEC Conservatives, entering a ready-made low-tariff market in Europe seemed the best way to revitalize the economy without experimenting with high-risk and potentially "socialist" thinking.

Advocating cooperation in Europe also drew on a Liberal tradition of scepticism about the idea of national "sovereignty". In 1918, Edward, now Viscount, Grey, defended the idea of a League of Nations to restrain militarism and bullying of weak states by strong ones. All countries must accept "some limitation upon the national action of each" and agree to send disputes to conference, conciliation and arbitration (Grey 1918: 8–9). The League would also end secret diplomacy, a traditional Liberal bugbear. As economic nationalism returned during the Depression, Walter Layton and Ramsay Muir presented the interdependency of nations as the political equivalent of international free trade. Muir, the president of the NLF, insisted that the Liberal principle that freedom needed regulation by law applied equally to the international arena, and that the duty of the League was to "outlaw war" (Muir 1934: 14). At the 1937 Liberal Party Assembly, he urged international agreement to determine colonial boundaries and access to colonial raw materials (Grayson 2001: 147–8). In *The Liberal Future* in 1959, Grimond argued that sovereign state boundaries were "dangerous anachronisms" transcended by modern financial and defensive requirements, but that patriotism was also a real human need, so that the essential partnerships of the future needed to grow organically from existing cultural ties. Britain's connections with the Commonwealth, Europe and the United States would all help to develop international cooperation (Grimond 1959: 157–69).

The small band of Liberal MPs played a disproportionately significant role in the passage of the bill to approve entry to the EEC in 1972: the second reading, and some later votes, passed narrowly because all but one of them were in support. Entry did not settle the question, as the 1974 Labour government called a referendum to confirm the decision. The European debates of the 1970s focused on the severe economic and political challenges that Britain faced and the benefits of some degree of international cooperation to meet them. Advocates of EEC entry argued that Britain would have more control over its destiny in partnership than by going it alone in a world of food shortages and of oil supplies controlled by the Organization of the Petroleum Exporting Countries (Saunders 2018: 231–53). The Liberal academic William Wallace suggested that the idea of untrammelled national autonomy was a fantasy in the modern world. International cooperation in NATO and the EEC strengthened not just Britain's security but also its freedom of manoeuvre. The European Community could secure better bargains in trade negotiations than Britain alone, protecting British manufacturing from competition from developing countries and strengthening Europe's hand in dealing with the Middle Eastern oil cartel (Wallace 1979).

Paddy Ashdown

Contributor: The Independent/Alamy Stock Photo.

In this national debate, among the keenest advocates of "sovereignty" were left-wing Labour MPs hostile not just to liberal ideas of international political cooperation but also to liberal capitalism itself. So the case for Europe became bound up with hostility to their case that the postwar economic order had failed and should give way to "socialism in one country". Europe became the best indicator of a politician's commitment to the centrist economic approach discussed in Chapter 4. Throughout these debates, and especially during the 1975 referendum on British membership, Liberal MPs cooperated with the pro-European faction of Labour MPs led by Roy Jenkins, paving the way for the SDP–Liberal Alliance in 1981.

In the 1990s, the role of NATO in humanitarian peacekeeping in the Balkans further increased the attractiveness of international institutions to Liberals. Under the leadership of Ashdown and Russell Johnston, Lib Dems pushed hard for international intervention in Bosnia in the 1990s and in Kosovo in the 2000s, to end Serbian efforts to extinguish Bosnian independence and Kosovan autonomy. Meanwhile, the emergence of concerns about climate change underlined the importance of international cooperation: in March 1996, Ashdown claimed that faced with such issues, the idea that the world could be managed on principles of state sovereignty was "a nostalgic myth" (Russell 1999: 80).

The Maastricht Treaty of 1992 created the EU and paved the way for an optional European single currency. As in 1972, Lib Dem MPs had considerable influence on parliamentary voting on the treaty, in the face of Conservative backbench rebellions against John Major's government. At the 1997 election, the Lib Dems supported the adoption of the euro but also urged the importance of democratizing the EU, especially by increasing the accountability of the Council of Ministers to the European Parliament, which had been directly elected since 1979. In the 1997 Cook–Maclennan Agreement, Labour agreed – at the last minute – to strong Lib Dem pressure that PR should be used for future European elections in Britain, in a striking contrast to Callaghan's refusal to concede the same in 1978 (Ashdown 2000: 534–5). From 1999, European elections fought on PR gave the Lib Dems – and the concept of PR – a higher profile. In the 2004 election, they took 12 of the UK's 78 seats, on 14.4 per cent of the vote.

Liberalism and the Brexit crisis

In the 20 years up to 2015, the Lib Dems could feel that they were exercising more influence on national politics than at any time since the 1920s. Yet in the following decade, they experienced three bad election results, Britain's exit from the EU and a public discourse that was often extremely critical of "liberalism".

Growing public scepticism about EU membership was bound up with the waning of the specific strategic and economic fears that had propelled entry. In the 1990s, the end of the Cold War increased complacency about global peace and food supplies, and diminished Russia's threat to Europe. The British economy seemed to have recovered from its 1970s malaise, the intellectual challenge from socialism declined, and globalization made regional protection networks less necessary. Then the Blair, Brown and Cameron governments presided over a great increase in immigration from Europe, while the media feasted critically on the Home Office's serial difficulties in managing asylum seekers.

Between 2004 and 2014, the United Kingdom Independence Party (UKIP), led by Nigel Farage, developed into a major threat to the

Conservative Party. Paradoxically, it was the introduction of PR for European elections that exposed this threat. It grew steadily until it topped the poll in 2014 with 27 per cent of the vote. It argued that the EU was imposing swathes of bureaucratic legislation on Britain and making it impossible to restrict immigration: rejection of its pretensions was needed to maintain Britain's political independence and economic freedoms.

Readers may feel inclined to compare this movement to the liberal ones discussed in the previous pages: as a demand to resist over-mighty power and to relegitimize a complacent, even corrupt political system (particularly in the light of a serious MPs' expenses scandal in 2008–9). They may wonder whether Lib Dems were hypocritical in not showing more sympathy with it, or, more likely, whether my definitions are at fault.

To this argument, there are two answers. One is that the Lib Dems did acknowledge that the EU needed democratic reform and the repatriation of some powers to local level, in line with the subsidiarity clauses of the Maastricht Treaty. Party leader Nick Clegg made both arguments in the *Orange Book*. In retrospect, however, more might have been said. Tactically, Lib Dems downplayed the EU issue altogether: it hardly featured in the 2010 manifesto. They continued to suggest that international cooperation remained the best way to tackle the problems of climate change, cross-border terrorism and globalization, but this was not argued in much detail. Their experience of Europe also suggested to them that the EU was a more complex and less powerful entity than Eurosceptics claimed, and that Britain had as much influence over its deliberations as it could reasonably expect.

The other is that the Brexit crisis was caused less by ingrained public hostility to the EU than by politics. The rise of UKIP reflected the existential problem faced by the British right after the collapse of its main historic argument: the need to rally against the threat of socialism. It was not that the right lacked other available rallying cries: it had two. These were seductive, largely incompatible and very difficult to achieve given the limitations of the state apparatus. One was the further development of free market Thatcherism towards a free enterprise, low-tax Singaporean economic model. The other, which is sometimes summarized as "post-liberalism", was to marshal Britain's sovereign powers to pursue interventionist policies to rectify the poor state of public services, to help the "left behind" and to crack down on immigration and crime. Both visions involved so much ambitious political restructuring that they were better suited to insurgent movements than to governing parties. Cameron tried to deflate UKIP's bubble by declaring his willingness to hold a referendum on EU membership in 2016. In the campaign, Vote Leave's slogan of "Take Back Control" managed to tap the resentment, and the aspirations, of enough people in both camps to secure a narrow victory, hiding the tensions between them for the time being. Nigel Farage declared "Independence Day".

Moreover, the referendum itself made the Brexit crisis more unmanageable. Several referenda had been called on constitutional matters since 1975, but their function was usually confirmatory, as in 1975 on EEC membership and 1997 on devolution. On these occasions, the electorate was being given a limited choice: to block or to approve specific changes to British constitutional arrangements worked out by MPs. This was the referendum concept advocated by A. V. Dicey, the Liberal Unionist historian, before 1914. He argued, in vain, for a poll on any Irish Home Rule Act passed by parliament, claiming that it would give voters the chance to correct any errors made by party-based majority government (Dicey 1915: c).

The 2016 referendum, by contrast, was an invitation to voters to pronounce on the abstract aspirations to "Take Back Control". The Leave victory in the referendum forced government to try to deliver on those aspirations: to prioritize rejecting the grip of Brussels and regaining "sovereignty". In the years after the referendum, any government that seemed to fall short in those respects was berated by the Eurosceptic media for betraying the popular mandate. Yet "taking back control" was bound to fail as a political strategy, because absolute sovereignty would be economically damaging unless accompanied by a set of wholesale changes to the British state – broadly equating to the post-liberal vision – that the Conservative government had not planned to implement. Once Brexit had been achieved, the Conservatives were cornered. They felt obliged to boast that their function was to stop high immigration, help the "left behind" and support "levelling up", but they had no effective plans to do any of these things. The ideologization of Conservative discourse had trapped them into fighting a battle they could not win. This gave many openings for critics on the right – led by Suella Braverman within the party and Nigel Farage outside it – to complain at their inaction, adding to the sense of a divided and incompetent government. Having been the main force cajoling the Conservative Party into promising a utopian vision of Brexit, Farage became the greatest beneficiary of their inevitable failure to realize it.

Moreover, the case for Brexit did not take enough account of the close connections between British and continental economies in the single market, the appeal of Britain's EU membership to international business, the problem of the Irish land border and the practical difficulty of disentangling Britain from EU regulations. After the referendum result, many Remain MPs from all parties still believed that a substantial compromise deal with the EU, based around the single market and/or the customs union, was essential. The result was protracted parliamentary wrangling between June 2016 and December 2019, which damaged popular perceptions of the effectiveness of parliament and led to bitter press attacks on the Remainer "liberal elite" for apparently frustrating the Brexit process.

Naturally the Lib Dems, the party most united around Remain in the referendum, came in for a large share of this criticism. From June 2016, Tim Farron, the party leader, had demanded a second referendum to confirm the result, and declared that the party would oppose Brexit at the next election. It came second in the 2019 European elections with 20 per cent of the vote (during which Lib Dems publicized their policy by wearing "Bollocks to Brexit" T-shirts). In October, opinion polls suggested that 53 per cent of the public would now support Remain in another referendum. Meanwhile, the Labour Party, led by the left-wing MP Jeremy Corbyn, was also undergoing an internal crisis: in February 2019, eight of its MPs had resigned to form a group, later known as "Change UK", advocating a second referendum. Subsequently, three dissident pro-EU Conservative MPs joined it, and by the autumn, several of the Change MPs had joined the Lib Dems. All this encouraged the Lib Dems under their new leader Jo Swinson to feel confident about fighting an election on the principle of revoking EU departure. It might even have foreshadowed a realignment of politics, on the basis of Remain versus Leave. Lib Dem MPs' behaviour was instrumental in triggering an election in December 2019.

This was a bad miscalculation. Prime Minister Boris Johnson fought it on another ambiguous slogan, "Get Brexit Done". He gained a large majority. This was essentially a transactional decision by an electorate fed up with parliamentary infighting, and willing to give Johnson the chance to deliver the Brexit benefits he promised. It was also helped by Corbyn's electoral divisiveness. Although the Lib Dem share of the vote increased from 7.4 to 11.6 per cent, their number of seats fell, from 12 to 11, and Swinson lost her own seat.

Over the next five years, government was never able to "take back control". Brexit became associated with obstacles and extra costs. Growth did not materialize, hindered also by the immense disruptions caused by Covid-19 and the Ukraine war. Immigration rose sharply, as did the number of asylum seekers. Opinion polls began to indicate that most people now saw Brexit as a mistake. But it was still a very contentious and divisive subject. During the 2024 election campaign, the Labour Party was extremely reluctant to hint at reopening the essentials of the Brexit settlement.

The Lib Dems' manifesto pledges included rejoining the single market, although their rhetoric focused on domestic policy instead. Support for EU membership contributed to their appeal in 2024, since the Conservative Party had become unambiguously a Brexit party. Only 18 per cent of voters with a university degree voted Conservative in 2024 (McDonnell 2024). However, voter knowledge of parties' positions should not be overstated: an estimated 30 per cent of Lib Dem voters backed Leave in the 2016 referendum (Statista 2016).

If Labour's boasted "growth" and "delivery" do not show electoral benefits by the late 2020s, it is difficult to believe that momentum will not build in favour of rejoining the single market, on grounds very similar to those used to advocate joining the EEC in 1960–61. There will be an obvious incentive to pull the same "growth" lever that pro-European Liberals and Conservatives identified then, especially if that lever will also help to promote environmental policy and allow Europe to defend itself better against threats from the east. Lib Dems may also see this as another chance to promote party realignment. Yet Nigel Farage and the Reform Party are likely to mount a more aggressive attack on the two-party system, on very different grounds, by signalling their strong opposition to collaboration with, and immigration from, the EU. The prospects of party realignment, it appears, continue to be intimately bound up with "Europe".

Conclusion

The Introduction to this book suggested that the best way to define historical British political Liberalism is as a series of stances and campaigns against concentrations of power, with the aim of boosting good governance and individual freedom, in opposition to interest groups that wield too much political or social influence, or to institutional rigidities and shortcomings that require redress. Over-mighty interests may be located anywhere on the post-1920 political spectrum: Liberals have not felt imprisoned by a conventional left–right political model. International corporations may exert excessive power over our lives in some ways, at the same time as public sector unions and complacent bureaucracies do in others.

Some readers who have persevered this far may be persuaded by this claim, but others may feel that it is too generous to many of the politicians who have traded under the name Liberal. The history of Liberal parties has included periods not only of coherence and dynamism but also of consolidation, complacency or confusion. Some political strategies have succeeded but many have failed, from bad timing, judgement or luck. Some vested interests have turned out too strong for Liberals; others have persuaded the public that they are more useful than Liberals have claimed. Many Liberals have moderated their aspirations in the face of obstacles posed by Conservative electoral strength, institutional inertia or imperial strategic needs. And for long periods since the 1920s, the primary objective has simply been survival.

All political strategies have limited shelf lives. Even in the pre-1920 period, there were arguably only three Liberal leaders – Lord John Russell, William Gladstone and David Lloyd George – whose activist approach powerfully shaped the party's sense of itself, and none of these visions was without its problems. (The same could be said of a couple of others who influenced the party but never led it, such as Richard Cobden and Joseph Chamberlain.)

Russell was the most significant driving force in Liberal politics between 1828 and 1852, although several other politicians shared his agenda and led on aspects of it. The most important part of this project was the 1832 Reform Act and various accompanying constitutional adjustments to improve the reputation and efficiency of both the state and the Church. The aim was to renew aristocratic leadership in politics, and moral leadership in religion, by requiring both sets of leaders to engage with a broader political nation, and with modern ideas about governance, social reform and religious pluralism. Russell was viscerally opposed to the practice of Tory Anglican aristocratic politics, which he felt had had terrible effects on social relations, on political awareness, on the socialization of poor children, on civic trust between Anglicans and Nonconformists and on the prospects for Ireland within the Union. One major problem with his strategy was that few aristocrats and churchmen fitted his ideal, in Britain let alone in Ireland, so his proposals stirred up a lot of indignant Tory antagonism. In response, his increasingly fitful and unpredictable legislative enthusiasms seemed to his Liberal critics to fall between stools. They raised big issues that were best left alone unless they could be settled with the business-like confidence that Liberals had shown in dealing with crime, pauperism and Canada in the 1830s, but they failed to pacify radical townsmen, Nonconformists and Irishmen in the desperate conditions of the 1840s.

Gladstone's aims were fundamentally similar – by activist political leadership to defend propertied-class rule and the Anglican religion – but with different perspectives that reflected his Peelite Tory inheritance. His main concern before 1874 was to cleanse the administration and expense of the state so thoroughly that radicals could not claim that it was still a nest of vested class interests. This strategy of demonstrating state disinterestedness and probity also ensured his popularity with the Liberal rank-and-file in the 1860s, which propelled him to the premiership. Cobdenite radicals liked his zeal about tax-cutting, especially on defence spending, while his declaration in favour of the disestablishment of the Irish Church hinted that the principle of disinterestedness would be applied to the rest of Irish policy and to religious and educational questions in Britain. This won him friends in Ireland and among radical Nonconformists who hoped to promote a self-reliant national religious commonwealth through the separation of Church and state in Britain. In fact, Gladstone's objective was more conservative and limited: to kill the old destructive radical scepticism about the propertied political order and the Church of England. In general terms, he succeeded: after 1867, radicals became less hostile to the state apparatus, while the Nonconformist urban elites married increasing social conservatism with a switch away from disestablishment demands to moralized humanitarian campaigns for temperance or foreign causes. Nonetheless, the emergence of a mass party system from the 1870s made it inevitable that radical Liberals would carry on criticizing national institutions such as Church and monarchy, and that in this new, more forgiving climate, Conservatives would acquire popularity by defending them. In particular, Liberal cost-cutting in defence, and scepticism about empire, were bitterly attacked as unpatriotic and unrealistic in the 1880s and 1890s. Conservative charges that Liberals did not understand empire became even easier to make after Gladstone's dramatic declaration against the "force and fraud" of the Union with Ireland, for which Britain must atone and allow Ireland to find its own propertied leaders. Gladstone saw the Irish Home Rule question as an engine to secure principles of good government, in Britain as well as in Ireland. He argued this case through crusading but divisive popular speeches against those who stood in his way, invoking the judgement of "the masses against the classes".

Lloyd George was the most dynamic of the Edwardian Liberals who had to confront a major fiscal problem: the growing cost of defending British global power while meeting voter expectations to care for the old, the unemployed and Britain's potential soldiers. The Liberals also faced a deliberate attempt by Tories to challenge their raison d'être as an energetic political force, by using the House of Lords to block most of their reforms. Many Liberals were conventional politicians who quailed at overtly attacking the Lords, but Lloyd George was more single-minded and more consciously a social outsider. Even so, this was an attack on the Lords' *political* power, not on the social standing of the aristocracy: two of Asquith's sons married peers' daughters, while Lloyd George later became a prolific and imaginative bestower of peerages. His main concern was to modernize the tax system by requiring a substantially higher contribution from two powerful vested interest groups: antisocial landlords in town and country, and the capitalist plutocrats who had helped to drive imperialism. If they paid their fair share, they would leave the productive classes free to contribute to national economic success, as workers and spenders. His energetic ambition led him into a land campaign, and then into handling the war effort from 1914, which led to a coup against the less energetic Asquith. Lloyd George presided over victory in war and reformed the machinery of government; he saw himself as the obvious man to spearhead efficient postwar reconstruction. He may have hoped that the magnetism of success would draw to him supporters from all the old parties. But circumstances defeated him, and the Conservative and Labour parties spent much of the 1920s destroying what remaining threat he posed to them, although it was never likely that he could have stopped what after 1922 was an inexorable process of Liberal marginalization.

Martin Pugh once wrote that Lloyd George was not a Liberal in the sense of being interested in the defence of individual and constitutional freedoms (Pugh 1988: 188). However, if we define Liberalism instead as an energetic attack on specific evils and interests, with the intention of demonstrating the merit of the political process and of liberal capitalism, he offers a better fit. The *Yellow Book* of 1928 was not quite the heroic novelty that its advocates claimed, in philosophical terms, but it was an important rebuke to the stilted negativity of the other parties and a defiant reassertion of the need for an energetic and moralized politics if democracy was to flourish in economically uncertain times.

Subsequent attempts at party renewal have been constrained by the difficulty of escaping the bonds of third-party status. Jo Grimond attracted a lot of attention after 1956 by his reworking of the party agenda to address the problems that postwar Britain faced domestically and internationally. His suggestion that the two main parties were trapping Britain's economy in the past revitalized the Liberal cause but encountered the same fundamental problem as David Steel, Roy Jenkins and Paddy Ashdown did between the 1970s and 1990s: that popular discontent with one part of the two-party system was not then so fundamental that it could not be addressed successfully by the leader of the other party, in the shape of Thatcher and then Blair.

All these attempts to reinvigorate or renew the party's sense of purpose ran out of steam eventually. In contrast to these activist figures stand other Liberal leaders whose primary aim has been more defensive: to prevent party disintegration, to hold the political centre, to prevent the unleashing of radical energies that would frighten voters into Conservative arms. Several examples could be cited, particularly since the 1920s. In the nineteenth century, the most obvious figure of this type was Palmerston. He adopted and celebrated the standard Victorian Liberal positions: of free trade, low-cost administration and pride in Britain's liberal constitution. Most MPs during his heyday were happy to identify with these values and, like him, did not see further reform as a priority. But Palmerston still contributed something significant to the Liberal creed. He rejected Gladstone's zeal for economy in favour of the view that robust defence spending was the basis of British power abroad. He reinterpreted the old idea of a balance of power in Europe. His aim was to prevent the autocratic powers of eastern Europe from stopping constitutional regimes gradually taking root in the West, while teaching France, forcefully if necessary (as in the eastern crisis of 1840), to be Britain's subordinate partner in both West and East, rather than to resume its Napoleonic career of conquest. This vision of Britain using its naval power and political example to coax the more mature European peoples to wriggle free from Russo-Austrian oppression was politically effective at home for a long time but lost its plausibility from the 1870s. Now the continental empires dominated European diplomacy, while they and Britain scrambled to divide the rest of the world between them. Liberals never agreed on how to handle the resulting popular imperial sentiment at home.

Leaders do not always have the luxury of being able to choose their political strategies. In the 2010s and 2020s, however, politics has been in a state of flux and unpredictability, and this may throw up new possibilities for leadership. The extent of disillusion with the two main parties is much larger now than even in the 1980s. The vote share of the two major parties was 97 per cent in 1950, 90 per cent in 1970 and 78 per cent in 1992, but fell to 58 per cent in 2024, as voters experimented not just with the Lib Dems and Scottish and Welsh Nationalists but with Reform, the Greens and independents. The turnout at the 2024 general election was one of the lowest ever in peacetime, at 60 per cent of the electorate (matched only by that in 2001). Electoral volatility has also been on the rise: across the four elections from 2005 to 2017, around 60 per cent of voters switched parties at least once. Two-party dominance now rests on much weaker foundations that it did when Lloyd George launched the *Yellow Book* in 1928.

In the 2020s, the Reform Party has played a much bigger role than the Lib Dems in stirring up hostility to the two-party system. The populism on which Reform's appeal rests has struck deep roots throughout the West, tells a simple story about institutional failure and betrayal that is designed to resonate with many voters, and is well supported in the media. Reform currently boasts that it is the only party that knows how to improve our lives through political reform and the removal of the political establishment.

At first sight, the Lib Dems seem to be pursuing a more cautious strategy. The party has no shortage of detailed policies – there were 22 chapters in the party's 2024 manifesto – but has shied away from bolder statements of intent about national renewal. Its MPs are not chasing media attention as avidly as are Labour, the Conservatives and Reform. Their priority seems to be to consolidate their position in their own seats and on local councils. They would argue that securing a base and validating local political activity are themselves essential elements of a properly functioning democratic system. Nationally, the Starmer government has a large majority and there seems little immediate prospect of a political crisis.

Time will tell if the Lib Dems are able to launch an effective national campaign on the issue of cooperation with Europe. The election of Donald Trump as United States President in November 2024 has increased the risk that American policy may no longer support European economic or security interests. If Europe is threatened by significant American tariffs, or by a resurgent Russia after a Ukraine peace settlement, momentum may build for common action across the continent. In January 2025, Lib Dem leader Ed Davey urged that Britain should negotiate a new customs union with the EU, including a Youth Mobility Scheme, in order to remove the trade obstacles and extra regulations arising from Brexit and to pave the way for a future return to the European single market. He argued that rejoining a customs union would greatly boost Britain's commerce and help its construction programme and NHS staffing, but he also suggested that a common front with Europe would help the country in the event of tariff negotiations with a transactional American government – and give it a much stronger hand in those negotiations than the Brexit-supporting Conservative or Reform Parties could manage (Davey 2025). Davey is likely to use his freedom as an opposition leader to criticize a lot of

Trump's behaviour, and to attack the priorities of any British government or party that seeks to curry favour with him.

Whenever the opportunity arises for Liberals again to make a bold activist case for their creed, there is no shortage of history to help them to do so. This book has shown how on several occasions they have built on existing popular grievances and expanded them into a broader case for a dynamic politics. The most assertive Liberal reform movements have tried to harness people's anger at problems that directly affect their lives, by showing how the best way to solve them safely is through reinvigorating and reshaping political structures. Most voters are not interested in abstract issues of representation, but there have been times when they have been persuaded that the distribution of power needs attention, if real grievances are to be corrected, social and institutional imbalances redressed, or economic and security needs tackled. At several points, Liberals have tried to make the case that politics is a duty and an opportunity: to help us stumble towards a better balance between local, national and international power structures, the creativity of liberal capitalism, and the humanity and dignity of the individual.

Chronology

This Chronology is organized around successive leaders of the Liberal and Liberal Democrat Parties in the House of Commons, named in bold. Periods in government are indicated by italics. In 1830–34, 1835–41, 1865–6 and 1894–5, Liberal prime ministers sat in the House of Lords.

1830–34	**Viscount Althorp**
1830–34	*Earl Grey prime minister*
1831–2	Reform crisis, leading to passage of 1832 Reform Act and large majority at 1832 election
1833	abolition of slavery
1834	*resignation of Earl Grey over Irish Church appropriation; Lord Melbourne prime minister*
1834	Althorp succeeds his father as a peer; Lord John Russell succeeds him; King William IV dismisses government; Sir Robert Peel minority Conservative government
1834–55	**Lord John Russell**
1835–41	*Lord Melbourne returns as prime minister after 1835 election; Compact with Daniel O'Connell; government defeated at 1841 election*
1835	Municipal Corporations Act
1838–9	Anti-Corn Law League founded; Chartist Convention
1840	Union of Upper and Lower Canada
1841–6	Peel Conservative government; repeal of Corn Laws, fall of government and split in Conservative Party 1846

1845–7	Irish famine
1846–52	*Lord John Russell prime minister; Liberals gain seats at 1847 election but still depend for majority on Peelite and Irish MPs; Russell resigns early 1852 after dismissal of Palmerston*
1852	minority Conservative government (Lord Derby); no party majority at 1852 election
1852–5	*Liberal–Peelite coalition; Lord Aberdeen Peelite prime minister; government falls over war management*
1854–6	Crimean War
1855–65	**Viscount Palmerston**
1855–8	*Palmerston heads coalition; Peelites soon resign; Russell leaves government after failure of Vienna peace talks; clear Liberal majority at 1857 election but Palmerston defeated 1858 over legislation to help the French government to counter assassination attempts*
1857	Indian Rebellion
1858–9	minority Conservative government; its Reform Bill defeated; Liberal majority at 1859 election
1859–65	*Palmerston returns as prime minister; Russell returns as foreign secretary; Peelites return, with Gladstone as Chancellor of the Exchequer; strong Liberal majority at 1865 election; Palmerston dies in office October 1865*
1860	Anglo-French Commercial Treaty; Italian unification
1865–75	**William Gladstone**
1865–6	*Lord John Russell prime minister (as Earl Russell); government falls after its Reform Bill defeated*
1866–8	minority Conservative government (Lord Derby and then Benjamin Disraeli); passes 1867 Reform Bill; defeated on Gladstone's Irish Church resolutions 1868; strong Liberal majority at 1868 election
1868–74	*Gladstone prime minister; 1873 briefly resigns after Irish University Bill defeated; 1874 proposes abolition of income tax and dissolves parliament; Conservative majority at election*

1870	Franco-Prussian War
1874–80	Benjamin Disraeli Conservative prime minister
1875	Gladstone announces retirement as party leader
1875–80	**Marquess of Hartington**
1875	Hartington chosen by Liberal MPs as leader
1876	Ottoman killings in Bulgaria; Gladstone's pamphlet encourages Bulgarian Agitation
1877	National Liberal Federation founded by Joseph Chamberlain
1879	Land League founded in Ireland; "Land War" begins
1879–80	Gladstone mounts two high-profile speaking campaigns in his new constituency of Midlothian
1880	healthy Liberal majority at election; Hartington and Lord Granville decline Queen Victoria's request to form a Liberal government, recommending Gladstone
1880–94	**William Gladstone**
1880–85	*Gladstone prime minister; defeated by Conservatives with help of Irish MPs over 1885 budget*
1881–2	Irish Nationalist leader Parnell in prison, released 1882; forms National League
1882	British occupation of Egypt; Mahdist rebellion in Sudan and defeat of British troops 1883; General Gordon sent at head of relief force but is killed 1885
1884–5	Reform and Redistribution Acts
1885–6	minority Conservative government; 1885 election leaves Liberals just short of overall majority while Parnell's Nationalists dominate Ireland outside Ulster; Gladstone indicates willingness to consider Irish Home Rule; Conservative government defeated
1886	*Gladstone government; Hartington declines to serve; Chamberlain resigns once Home Rule plans announced; revolt of 94 Liberal MPs defeats Government of Ireland Bill; Gladstone calls election; Hartington, Chamberlain and colleagues fight as Liberal Unionists; Liberals badly defeated (192 seats); 77 Liberal Unionists*

1886–92	Conservative government
1891	National Liberal Federation conference at Newcastle produces policy programme
1892	Conservative government loses majority at election
1892–4	*Gladstone prime minister; Liberals depend on Irish Nationalists for majority; Government of Ireland Bill defeated by House of Lords 1893; Gladstone resigns 1894 after lack of cabinet support for his attempt to resist higher naval spending*
1894–8	**Sir William Harcourt**
1894–5	*Lord Rosebery prime minister; cabinet disunity; resigns 1895*
1895–1905	Conservative and Unionist governments; strong majority at 1895 election; Unionists in cabinet: Hartington (now Duke of Devonshire), Chamberlain, Goschen, Lansdowne, Henry James
1898	Harcourt retires as leader; Liberals split over imperialism
1899–1908	**Sir Henry Campbell-Bannerman**
1899–1902	Boer War; strong Conservative majority at 1900 election
1903	Liberal–Labour electoral pact
1903	Chamberlain declaration for Tariff Reform; Conservatives increasingly disunited; Balfour government falls 1905
1902	Anglo-Japanese Alliance; 1904 Anglo-French Entente
1905–8	*Campbell-Bannerman prime minister; landslide majority 1906 election; resigns April 1908 and dies that month*
1907	Anglo-Russian Entente negotiated by Foreign Secretary Edward Grey
1908–24	**Henry Asquith (out of parliament 1919–20; Donald Maclean interim leader)**
1908–16	*Henry Asquith prime minister*
1909–11	People's Budget and constitutional crisis over role of House of Lords; two general elections in 1910; Liberals lose majority, now dependent on Irish Nationalist and Labour MPs

1914	outbreak of First World War
1915	Dardanelles Campaign; munitions crisis; government reconstituted as coalition with eight Conservative cabinet ministers; Asquith criticized for delaying conscription
1916	mounting disquiet at lack of progress in war; November–December move against Asquith's leadership by Lloyd George and Conservatives, pressing for a small War Council; Asquith forced to resign
1916–22	*Lloyd George prime minister of coalition government; war ends November 1918; Lloyd George introduces Coupon for 1918 election; only 27 Liberal MPs returned outside the coalition; Conservatives dominant in coalition, remove Lloyd George 1922 and gain majority at election*
1918	Sinn Fein dominate elections in Ireland; war of independence; 1921 Anglo-Irish Treaty establishes Irish Free State and an opt-out for the six counties of Northern Ireland
1923–4	Conservative leader Baldwin seeks electoral mandate for protection; Asquith and Lloyd George reunite to fight for free trade at 1923 election; Liberals hold the balance of power and support minority Labour government of Ramsay MacDonald
1924	general election; Liberals reduced to 40 seats; Asquith loses seat, becomes Earl of Oxford, resigns overall party leadership 1926
1924–31	**David Lloyd George**
1926	General Strike
1929–31	minority Labour government, falls August 1931
1931–5	**Herbert Samuel**
1931–2	*National Government with support of Liberals and of Liberal Nationals who establish separate organization under Sir John Simon*
1932–40	National Government continues; Liberal Nationals stay in office, but Samuel's supporters leave in 1932 over imperial preference
1935–45	**Sir Archibald Sinclair**

1940–5	*Sinclair in Churchill wartime coalition government as secretary of state for air*
1945–56	**Clement Davies**
1956–67	**Jo Grimond**
1958	Torrington by-election victory
1959–60	Liberal Party commits to support EEC membership
1962	Orpington by-election victory
1967–76	**Jeremy Thorpe**
1972–3	five by-election victories
1974	Thorpe rejects offer from Edward Heath of a cabinet post after February election returns a hung parliament
1976	Thorpe resigns after press coverage of a plot to murder Norman Scott
1976–88	**David Steel**
1977–8	Liberal pact to support minority Labour government in return for some consultation on policy
1979	Liverpool Edge Hill by-election victory
1981	formation of Social Democratic Party (SDP) and SDP–Liberal Alliance
1981–7	four by-election victories
1988	merger as Social and Liberal Democrats
1988–99	**Paddy Ashdown**
1989	party name changed to Liberal Democrats (Lib Dems)
1990–91	three by-election victories
1992–7	four by-election victories
1996–7	Joint Consultative Committee on Constitutional Reform and Cook–Maclennan Agreement

1999–2006	**Charles Kennedy**
1999–2007	*Labour–Lib Dem coalition government in Scotland*
2003	Iraq War
2000–6	four by-election victories
2006–7	**Menzies Campbell**
2007–15	**Nick Clegg**
2010–15	*Conservative–Lib Dem coalition government; Clegg deputy prime minister; five Lib Dem cabinet ministers; party reduced from 57 to 8 seats at 2015 election*
2015–17	**Tim Farron**
2016	Brexit referendum
2016	Richmond Park by-election gain
2017–19	**Vince Cable**
2019	Brecon and Radnorshire by-election gain
2019	**Jo Swinson**
2020–	**Ed Davey**
2021–3	four by-election gains
2024	General election campaign produces a postwar record of 72 Lib Dem MPs

Further reading

Barberis, P. 2005. *Liberal Lion: Jo Grimond, A Political Life*. London: I. B.Tauris.

Bernstein, G. 1986. *Liberalism and Liberal Politics in Edwardian England*. London: Allen & Unwin.

Biagini, E. 1999. *Gladstone*. New York: St Martin's Press.

Dutton, D. 2012. *A History of the Liberal Party since 1900*. Basingstoke: Palgrave Macmillan.

Fawcett, E. 2015. *Liberalism: The Life of an Idea*. Princeton, NJ: Princeton University Press.

Howe, A. 1997. *Free Trade and Liberal England, 1846–1946*. Oxford: Oxford University Press.

Parry, J. 1993. *The Rise and Fall of Liberal Government in Victorian Britain*. New Haven, CT: Yale University Press.

Pugh, M. 1988. *Lloyd George*. Harlow: Longman.

Searle, G. 2001. *The Liberal Party: Triumph and Disintegration, 1886–1929*. Basingstoke: Palgrave Macmillan.

Sloman, P. 2015. *The Liberal Party and the Economy, 1929–1964*. Oxford: Oxford University Press.

Bibliography

This list includes all works referenced in the text, except where the textual reference is already adequate. I have not supplied references to texts that can easily be found on the internet. This includes party election manifestoes.

Ashdown, P. 2000. *The Ashdown Diaries*, Vol. 1, *1988–1997*. London: Allen Lane.

Ashdown, P. 2001. "Ashdown as leader". Interview. *Journal of Liberal History* 30.

Baines, M. 2004. "Liberals and Europe". *Journal of Liberal History* 42.

Bebbington, D. 1982. *The Nonconformist Conscience: Chapel and Politics 1870–1914*. London: Allen & Unwin.

Bentley, M. 1974. "The liberal response to socialism, 1918–29". In K. Brown (ed.), *Essays in Anti-Labour History*. London: Macmillan.

Bernstein, G. 1986. *Liberalism and Liberal Politics in Edwardian England*. London: Allen & Unwin.

Blair, T. 2010. *A Journey*. London: Hutchinson.

Blewett, N. 1972. *The Peers, the Parties and the People: The General Elections of 1910*. London: Macmillan.

Brack, D., R. Grayson & D. Howarth 2007. *Reinventing the State: Social Liberalism for the 21st Century*. London: Politico's.

Braverman, S. 2024. "Suella delivers speech in Washington DC at the National Conservatism Conference". 8 July. https://www.suellabraverman.co.uk/news/suella-delivers-speech-washington-dc-national-conservatism-conference.

Brent, R. 1987. "The Whigs and Protestant Dissent in the decade of reform: the case of church rates, 1833–1841". *English Historical Review*, 102(405): 897–910.

Brown, G. 2006. "Speech to the Fabian New Year Conference, London 2006". British Political Speech. http://www.britishpoliticalspeech.org/speech-archive.htm?speech=316.

Buckner, P. 1985. *The Transition to Responsible Government: British Policy in British North America, 1815–1850*. Westport, CT: Greenwood.

Butler, D. 1952. *The British General Election of 1951*. London: Macmillan.

Butler, D. & D. Kavanagh 1997. *The British General Election of 1997*. Basingstoke: Palgrave Macmillan.

Cain, P. 1979. "Capitalism, war and internationalism in the thought of Richard Cobden". *Review of International Studies* 5(3): 229–47.

Calkins, W. 1960. "A Victorian free trade lobby". *Economic History Review* 13(1): 90–104.

Claeys, G. 2010. *Imperial Sceptics: British Critics of Empire, 1850–1920*. Cambridge: Cambridge University Press.

Clarke, P. 1975. "The electoral position of the Liberal and Labour Parties, 1910–1914". *English Historical Review* 90(357): 828–36.

Coohill, J. 2011. *Ideas of the Liberal Party: Perceptions, Agendas and Liberal Politics in the House of Commons, 1832–52*. Chichester: Wiley-Blackwell.

Daunton, M. 2001. *Taxing Leviathan: The Politics of Taxation in Britain, 1799–1914*. Cambridge: Cambridge University Press.

Davey, E. 2025. "Britain leading again". 16 January. British Political Speech. https://www.libdems.org.uk/news/article/britain-leading-again.

Deacon, R. 2005–6. "The slow death of Liberal Wales 1906–1979". *Journal of Liberal History* 49.

Deacon, R. 2014. "Going into Labour: the Welsh Liberal Democrat coalition experience". *Journal of Liberal History* 83.

Deneen, P. 2018. *Why Liberalism Failed*. New Haven, CT: Yale University Press.

Dewey, C. 1974. "Celtic agrarian legislation and the Celtic revival: historicist implications of Gladstone's Irish and Scottish Land Acts, 1870–86". *Past & Present* 64: 30–70.

Dicey, A. 1915. *Introduction to the Study of the Law of the Constitution*. London: Macmillan.

Dickinson, J. 1853. *India: Its Government under a Bureaucracy*. London: Saunders & Stanford.

Douglas, R. 2005. *Liberals: A History of the Liberal and Liberal Democrat Parties*. London: Hambledon.

Dutton, D. 2007. "Liberal Nationals". In D. Brack & E. Randall (eds), *Dictionary of Liberal Thought*. London: Politico's.

Dutton, D. 2012. *A History of the Liberal Party since 1900*. Basingstoke: Palgrave Macmillan.

Egan, M. 1997–8. "Harry Willcock: the forgotten champion of liberalism". *Journal of Liberal Democrat History* 17.

Elkins, C. 2022. *Legacy of Violence: A History of the British Empire*. London: Bodley Head.

Emy, H. 1973. *Liberals, Radicals and Social Politics 1892–1914*. Cambridge: Cambridge University Press.

Enright, A. 2022. *Charles Owen O'Conor, the O'Conor Don*. Dublin: Four Courts.

Fawcett, E. 2015. *Liberalism: The Life of an Idea*. Princeton, NJ: Princeton University Press.

Finnie, R. 2011. "Russell Johnston". *Journal of Liberal History* 71.

Freeden, M. 1989. *Minutes of the Rainbow Circle, 1894–1924*. London: Royal Historical Society.

Freeden, M. 2015. *Liberalism: A Very Short Introduction*. Oxford: Oxford University Press.

Fukuyama, F. 2024. "What Trump unleashed means for America". *Financial Times*, 8 November.

Fulford, R. 1959. *The Liberal Case*. Harmondsworth: Penguin.

Gailey, A. 2016. *The Lost Imperialist: Lord Dufferin, Memory and Mythmaking in an Age of Celebrity*. London: John Murray.

Goldman, L. 2006. "The defection of the middle class: the Endowed Schools Act, the Liberal Party, and the 1874 election". In P. Ghosh & L. Goldman (eds), *Politics and Culture in Victorian Britain: Essays in Memory of Colin Matthew*. Oxford: Oxford University Press.

Goodhart, D. 2012. "A post-liberal future?" Demos. https://demos.co.uk/wp-content/uploads/files/apostliberalfuture.pdf.

Gray, P. 1999. *Famine, Land and Politics: British Government and Irish Society, 1843–1850*. Dublin: Irish Academic Press.

Grayson, R. 2001. *Liberals, International Relations and Appeasement: The Liberal Party, 1919–1939*. London: Routledge.

Grey, E. 1918. *The League of Nations*. New York: George H. Doran.

Griffin, B. forthcoming. *The Gender Order and the Judicial Imagination*.

Grimond, J. 1959. *The Liberal Future*. London: Faber & Faber.

Grimond, J. 1963. *The Liberal Challenge*. London: Hollis & Carter.

Hamer, D. 1978. "Gladstone: the making of a political myth". *Victorian Studies* 22: 29–50.

Handcock, W. 1977. *English Historical Documents, 1874–1914*. London: Eyre & Spottiswoode.

Hansard's Parliamentary Debates [references in text supply relevant date and column numbers].

Harling, P. 1996. *The Waning of "Old Corruption": The Politics of Economical Reform in Britain, 1779–1846*. Oxford: Clarendon Press.

Harris, J. 1983. "The transition to high politics in English social policy, 1880–1914". In M. Bentley & J. Stevenson (eds), *High and Low Politics in Modern Britain: Ten Studies*. Oxford: Clarendon Press.

Harrison, B. 1970. "The British prohibitionists, 1853–72: a biographical analysis". *International Review of Social History* 15(3): 375–467.

Harvie, C. 1976. *The Lights of Liberalism: University Liberals and the Challenge of Democracy, 1860–86*. London: Allen Lane.

Hennock, E. 1973. *Fit and Proper Persons: Ideal and Reality in 19th Century Urban Government*. London: Edward Arnold.

Hickson, K. 2009. *The Political Thought of the Liberals and Liberal Democrats since 1945*. Manchester: Manchester University Press.

Hobhouse, L. 1911. *Liberalism*. London: Williams & Norgate.

Howarth, D. 2007. "What is Social Liberalism?". In D. Brack, R. Grayson & D. Howarth (eds), *Reinventing the State*. London: Politico's.

Howarth, D. 2014. "The Liberal Democrats and the functions of policy". *Journal of Liberal History* 83.

Howe, A. 1997. *Free Trade and Liberal England, 1846–1946*. Oxford: Oxford University Press.

Hunter, I. 2004. "Sir Archibald Sinclair: the Liberal anti-appeaser". *Journal of Liberal History* 42.

Jackson, A. 2003. *Home Rule: An Irish History, 1800–2000*. London: Weidenfeld & Nicolson.

Jalland, P. 1979. "United Kingdom devolution 1910–1914: political panacea or tactical diversion?". *English Historical Review* 94: 757–85.

Jones, S. 2024. "The Owens College Extension of 1870–3: rethinking the origins of the civic university tradition in England". *Bulletin of the John Rylands Library* 100(2): 53–74.

Jones, T. 1951. *Lloyd George*. Cambridge, MA: Harvard University Press.

Jones, T. 2011. *The Revival of British Liberalism: From Grimond to Clegg*. Basingstoke: Palgrave Macmillan.

Keeling, P. 2018. *British Liberal Internationalism in Retreat: The Channel Tunnel Controversy and the Naval Defence Act, 1880–1894*. PhD dissertation, University of Kent.

Kennedy, C. 2003, "The Liberal Democrat leader's address to his party conference in Brighton". *The Guardian*, 25 September. https://www.theguardian.com/politics/2003/sep/25/libdems2003.liberaldemocrats1.

Kerr, D. 1994. *"A Nation of Beggars"? Priests, People, and Politics in Famine Ireland, 1846–1852*. Oxford: Clarendon Press.

Keynes, J. 1931. *Essays in Persuasion*. London: Macmillan.

Kidd, C. 2008. *Unions and Unionisms: Political Thought in Scotland, 1500–2000*. Cambridge: Cambridge University Press.

Knights, M. 2021. *Trust and Distrust: Corruption in Office in Britain and Its Empire, 1600–1850*. Oxford: Oxford University Press.

Larsen, T. 1999. *Friends of Religious Equality: Nonconformist Politics in Mid-Victorian England*. Woodbridge: Boydell.

Lawrence, J. 2009. *Electing Our Masters: The Hustings in British Politics from Hogarth to Blair*. Oxford: Oxford University Press.

Laws, D. & P. Marshall 2004. *The Orange Book: Reclaiming Liberalism*. London: Profile.

Liberal Democrat History Group 2016. "Coalition and the Liberal Democrats: the policy record". *Journal of Liberal History* 92, special issue.

Lindsay, C. 2014. "Liberal Democrats in coalition: the Scottish record". *Journal of Liberal History* 83.

Loughlin, J. 1986. *Gladstone, Home Rule and the Ulster Question 1882–93*. Dublin: Gill & Macmillan.

MacColl, A. 2006. *Land, Faith and the Crofting Community: Christianity and Social Criticism in the Highlands of Scotland 1843–1893*. Edinburgh: Edinburgh University Press.

Machin, G. 1977. *Politics and the Churches in Great Britain 1832 to 1868*. Oxford: Clarendon Press.

Mandler, P. 1990. *Aristocratic Government in the Age of Reform: Whigs and Liberals, 1830–1852*. Oxford: Clarendon Press.

Mantena, K. 2010. *Alibis of Empire: Henry Maine and the Ends of Liberal Imperialism*. Princeton, NJ: Princeton University Press.

McDonnell, A. 2024. "How Britain voted in the 2024 general election". YouGov, 8 July. https://yougov.co.uk/politics/articles/49978-how-britain-voted-in-the-2024-general-election.

Meadowcroft, J. 1995. *Conceptualizing the State: Innovation and Dispute in British Political Thought, 1880–1914*. Oxford: Clarendon Press.

Mehta, U. 1999. *Liberalism and Empire: A Study in Nineteenth-Century British Liberal Thought*. Chicago: University of Chicago Press.

Miall, A. 1884. *Life of Edward Miall*. London: Macmillan.

Milbank, J. & A. Pabst 2016. *The Politics of Virtue: Post-Liberalism and the Human Future*. London: Rowman & Littlefield.

Mitchell, J. 2014. *The Scottish Question*. Oxford: Oxford University Press.

Moulton, E. 1968. *Lord Northbrook's Indian Administration, 1872–1876*. New York: Asia Publishing.

Muir, R. 1934. *The Liberal Way: A Survey of Liberal Policy*. London: Allen & Unwin.

Munson, J. 1991. *The Nonconformists: In Search of a Lost Culture*. London: SPCK.

Murray, B. 1980. *The People's Budget 1909/10: Lloyd George and Liberal Politics*. Oxford: Clarendon Press.

O'Day, A. 1979. "Irish Home Rule and liberalism". In A. O'Day (ed.), *The Edwardian Age: Conflict and Stability*. Basingstoke: Macmillan.

Offer, A. 1981. *Property and Politics 1870–1914: Landownership, Law, Ideology and Urban Development in England.* Cambridge: Cambridge University Press.

Pabst, A. 2017. "Postliberalism: the new centre ground of British politics". *Political Quarterly* 88(3): 500–9.

Packer, I. 2001. *Lloyd George, Liberalism and the Land: The Land Issue and Party Politics in England, 1906–1914*. Woodbridge: Boydell.

Parry, J. 1986. *Democracy and Religion: Gladstone and the Liberal Party, 1867–1875*. Cambridge: Cambridge University Press.

Parry, J. 1993. *The Rise and Fall of Liberal Government in Victorian Britain*. New Haven, CT: Yale University Press.

Parry, J. 1996. "Past and future in the later career of Lord John Russell". In T. Blanning & D. Cannadine (eds), *History and Biography: Essays in Honour of Derek Beales*. Cambridge: Cambridge University Press.

Parry, J. 2001. "The impact of Napoleon III on British politics, 1851–1880". *Transactions of the Royal Historical Society* 11, sixth series: 147–75.

Parry, J. 2001–2. "Lord John Russell and the Irish Catholics, 1829–1852". *Journal of Liberal Democrat History* 33.

Parry, J. 2006. *The Politics of Patriotism: English Liberalism, National Identity and Europe, 1830–1886*. Cambridge: Cambridge University Press.

Parry, J. 2011. "The decline of institutional reform in nineteenth-century Britain". In D. Feldman & J. Lawrence (eds), *Structures and Transformations in Modern British History*. Cambridge: Cambridge University Press.

Parry, J. 2017. "1867 and the rule of wealth". In R. Saunders (ed.), *Shooting Niagara – and After? The Second Reform Act and Its World*. Chichester: Wiley-Blackwell.

Parry, J. 2018. "Gladstone's first government: a policy overview". *Journal of Liberal History* 101.

Parry, J. 2024. "The Third Earl Grey, liberalism, and the British Empire". *Modern Intellectual History* 21(2): 239–68.

Partridge, M. 1989. *Military Planning for the Defense of the United Kingdom, 1814–1870*. New York: Greenwood.

Petrie, M. 2022. *Politics and the People: Scotland, 1945–1979*. Edinburgh: Edinburgh University Press.

Pugh, M. 1978. *Electoral Reform in War and Peace, 1906–18*. London: Routledge.

Pugh, M. 1980. *Women's Suffrage in Britain, 1867–1928*. London: Historical Association.

Pugh, M. 1988. *Lloyd George*. Harlow: Longman.

Rallings, C. & M. Thrasher 2007. *British Electoral Facts 1832–2006*. Aldershot: Ashgate.

Read, C. 2022. *The Great Famine in Ireland and Britain's Financial Crisis*. Woodbridge: Boydell.

Richter, M. 1964. *The Politics of Conscience: T. H. Green and His Age*. London: Weidenfeld & Nicolson.

Roberts, M. 2004. *Making English Morals: Voluntary Association and Moral Reform in England, 1787–1886*. Cambridge: Cambridge University Press.

Russell, C. 1999. *An Intelligent Person's Guide to Liberalism*. London: Duckworth.

Russell, J. 1870. *Selections from Speeches 1817 to 1841 and from Despatches 1859 to 1865*, 2 vols. London: Longmans.

Russell, G. 1883. "A protest against Whiggery". In *The Nineteenth Century: A Monthly Review*, Vol. 13 (January–June), 920–7. London: Kegan Paul, Trench & Co.

Särlvik, B. & I. Crewe 1983. *Decade of Dealignment: The Conservative Victory of 1979 and Electoral Trends in the 1970s*. Cambridge: Cambridge University Press.

Saunders, R. 2013. "Democracy". In D. Craig & J. Thompson (eds), *Languages of Politics in Nineteenth-Century Britain*. Basingstoke: Palgrave Macmillan.

Saunders, R. 2018. *Yes to Europe! The 1975 Referendum and Seventies Britain*. Cambridge: Cambridge University Press.

Scherer, P. 1999. *Lord John Russell: A Biography*. Selinsgrove, PA: Susquehanna University Press.

Schroeder, P. 1994. *The Transformation of European Politics, 1763–1848*. Oxford: Clarendon Press.

Searle, G. 1971. *The Quest for National Efficiency: A Study in British Politics and Political Thought, 1899–1914*. Oxford: Blackwell.

Searle, G. 1983. "The Edwardian Liberal Party and business". *English Historical Review* 98(386): 28–60.

Searle, G. 1987. *Corruption in British Politics 1895–1930*. Oxford: Clarendon Press.

Searle, G. 2004. *A New England? Peace and War 1886–1918*. Oxford: Clarendon Press.

Sell, G. 1997–8. "Scottish devolution: the Grimond years". *Journal of Liberal Democrat History* 17.

Semmel, B. 1962. *The Governor Eyre Controversy*. London: MacGibbon & Kee.

Shannon, R. 1963. *Gladstone and the Bulgarian Agitation 1876*. London: Nelson.

Shannon, R. 2007. *Gladstone: God and Politics*. London: Bloomsbury.

Sloman, P. 2015. *The Liberal Party and the Economy, 1929–1964*. Oxford: Oxford University Press.

Sloman, P. 2022. "'Take Power – Vote Liberal': Jeremy Thorpe, the 1974 Liberal revival, and the politics of 1970s Britain". *English Historical Review* 137(588): 1462–92.

Spychal, M. 2024. *Mapping the State: English Boundaries and the 1832 Reform Act*. London: University of London Press.

Statista 2016. "Which way did you vote in the Brexit referendum?" https://www.statista.com/statistics/518474/eu-referendum-voting-intention-by-political-affiliation/.

Steel, D. 1989. *Against Goliath*. London: Weidenfeld & Nicolson.

Sunderland, H. 2020. "Politics in schoolgirl debating cultures in England, 1886–1914". *Historical Journal* 63(4): 935–57.

Trentmann, F. 2008. *Free Trade Nation: Commerce, Consumption and Civil Society in Modern Britain*. Oxford: Oxford University Press.

Trevelyan, G. 1914. *The Life of John Bright*. London: Constable.

Wallace, W. 1979. *The Illusion of Sovereignty*. London: Liberal Publications Department.

Watson, G. 1957. *The Unservile State: Essays in Liberty and Welfare*. London: Allen & Unwin.

Whiting, C. 2024. "A triumph on tenuous ground". Liberal Democrat Voice, 9 July. https://www.libdemvoice.org/a-triumph-on-tenuous-ground-75617.html.

Williams, M. 2017. "What's Tim Farron's track record on LGBT rights?" Channel 4 News FactCheck, 26 April. https://www.channel4.com/news/factcheck/whats-tim-farrons-track-record-on-lgbt-rights.

Index